Also by Steven E

1994
Wake Up
An Inspirational Handbook

2001
Wake Up...Live the Life You Love
(First Edition)

2002
Wake Up...Live the Life You Love
(Second Edition)

2003
Wake Up...Shape Up...Live the Life You Love

2003
Wake Up...Live the Life You Love: Inspirational How-to Stories

2004
Wake Up...Live the Life You Love In Beauty

2004
Wake Up...Live the Life You Love, Living on Purpose

Wake Up...Live the Life You Love,

Wake Up Life the Life You Love
Finding Your Life's Passion

By Steven E and Lee Beard

and more than 50 of the world's top counselors and motivators

Wake Up...Live the Life You Love,

Published by:
Little Seed Publishing, LLC.
P.O. Box 4483
Laguna Beach, CA 92652

COPYRIGHT 2004 by Global Partnership, LLC

Pre-Press Management by TAE Marketing Consultations
Robert Valentine, Publication Director; Erin Forte, Senior Editor
and Public Relations; Adam Mathis, Assistant Editor;
Jennie Crawford, Editorial Assistant
Text Design: Klansee Bell

Cover Illustrations: Klansee Bell

All contributors acknowledge that they own or have
all necessary consents to use submitted materials.

Publisher intends this material for entertainment and no legal, medical
or other professional advice is implied or expressed. If the purchaser
cannot abide by this statement, please return the book for a full refund.

Acknowledgement is made for permission to quote copyrighted materials.

Distributed by Seven locks Press
3100 W. Warner Ave. #8
Santa Ana, CA 92704

Library of Congress Cataloguing-In-Publication Data
ISBN: 0-9644706-7-5

$14.95 USA   **$24.95 Canada**

Dedication

Dedication is pursuing through trials and
failures; it is looking ahead to the light when
the present seems so dark. Dedication is
finding your passion amid rising chaos.
It is dedication "combined with an intense,
courageous passion that shines from these pages."

To all of our co-authors, "this book is
dedicated with admiration and wonder."

Steven E and Lee Beard

*How would you like to be in the next book
with a fabulous group of best-selling authors?
Another Wake Up book is coming soon!*

*Visit:
WakeUpLive.com*

Additional author information can be found at:

*We would like to provide you with a free
gift to enhance this book experience.
For your free gift, please visit:
WakeUpGift.com*

Contents

Introduction

Some say passion is the essence of the soul. Passion is part of all of us. It fills our hearts and guides us to our purpose.

Passion is what fuels us as we travel down the road called life. Passion fills the road with amazing, fulfilling and successful stops along the way. It is our passion that seeks out our purpose among the stops.

Finding your purpose in life is fulfilling in itself, but if you are passionate about your purpose, you are on fire. The fire can spread.

This book is full of stories from best-selling authors, doctors, success coaches, financial experts and marketing consultants. These stories combine to complete our mission – our task – to show everyone how passion leads to a successful, fulfilled life.

It is our belief that you have fulfilled part of your purpose by opening this book; you are meant to live with passion.

Let us share our stories of starting over, listening to our hearts, overcoming obstacles and finding our passion. Let us guide you in your search for success fueled and sustained by the energy called passion.

Steven E and Lee

Manifesting
Steven E.

*L*et me explain how this works. We all have experienced a time when we thought of something and "bang" there it was. A thought in the mind and it becomes a material item. Everything you see was first a thought and then it became the chair that you are sitting on, or a pencil or a table. Everything is conceived before it becomes a physical object. Manifesting used to be this metaphysical concept that was not easy to explain. An example of this is seen when a quantum physicist is looking at the smallest particle. It appears, at first, in a hazy wave state. However, if he/she puts their concentration or observation on it, it will become a solid particle.

We live in a world where we see everything as being solid, but it is not solid at all. Even a rock, when it is broken down to its smallest particle, is in a hazy wave state. Now let me explain how you can put this into action. First, whatever we concentrate on will become more of our reality. If we want more health and a pain-free body, but we concentrate on how our back always hurts, we will get more pain. What we concentrate on will become greater. Keep your mind focused on your health, rather than lack of energy. Focus on the money that you do have, rather than that which you do not have.

Get a journal and begin writing about all the good you have. Each day write down things for which you are thankful. Concentrate on the things that you desire and watch them manifest into your life. Start learning about money; whose portrait is on the one, five, ten, twenty, fifty and hundred dollar bills. Treat money with respect as you would respect your health or family. Learn about the stock market and real estate. Buy books about people who have wealth. Get it out of your mind that money is bad, or it's evil. Money isn't evil. It's only a piece of paper!

You can be a loving, spiritual person, with plenty of money to share with your family and friends, or with worthy causes. Use your concentration and observation on money, happiness, health, love or whatever you desire, and watch the hazy wave particle turn into a solid form.

— Steven E

Adding Years to Your Life and Life to Your Years
Scott Conard, MD

You never forget the blank stare of a person without purpose. I remember looking into the eyes of my elderly patients, wondering what had happened. How could it have been different?

"How are you today?" I would ask.

"Fine," was always the reply.

"Are you in pain? Can I do anything to help you?"

"No."

"Have you been more active and started eating any better since I saw you last?"

"No."

"Is there anything I can do to encourage you to start being more active?"

"Leave me alone."

"OK, nice to see you."

After a few hours, my nursing home rounds would be done, and I would head to my office to see my "regular" patients.

That's how it went day after day. It didn't take long before I realized that my fresh-out-of medical school mission, "to add years to your life," was not enough. I began to contact letters their children to ask, "Can I care for you?" My mission changed. It was now "to add years to your life and life to your years!" I wanted to capture them while their spirit was intact to enhance and nourish it.

Many only came in when they felt pain. Often it was too late when cancer, heart disease, or osteoporosis struck. Condemned to the same fate as their parents, they had forgotten that we are meant to be a human "being." Using the system as an "illness care" system rather than a "health care" system, it often turned out to be a "too-late-to-care" system.

Some made their annual exams. Vigilant to look for "early disease," we screened for cancer and heart disease, intervening before it caused too many problems. I would see them for 20 to 30 minutes for the annual exam and another 15 minutes sometime during the year. They began to open their minds to early detection and prevention of disease. The "illness care system" had evolved into an "early detection" care system; but still not a "health care" system.

Finally, it happened! A patient watched his/her mom progress through the heart-wrenching steps of dying in a human warehouse. "Dr. Conard, you must help me take control of my health. I will not go through what my mom did. Please teach me how to live life to realize the best life possible; to reach my 'genetic potential,' to fulfill my purpose as long as possible." Finally, I was able to fulfill my purpose; I sat dumbfounded; so much to share, how do I do it? Developing a "health care system" meant another change of the mission: "adding years to your life and life to your years, by empowering you to take control of your health!"

An effective, supportive and personalized health care program to be delivered in a cost effective manner; how is it possible? I had to get people in The Game of Health™ to help them get around the bases, take control of their health and to learn and live the principles of The Seven Healers™. Their teammates were in the game – ready to assist in any health challenge they confront. They began experiencing the resolution of their health problems.

As they went through the program, the sparkle returned to their eyes, and they began to feel the flow of vitality. Energized for the first time in years, they considered the unlimited possibilities life had to offer. Soon un-diabetics joined the un-obese, the un-depressed and the un-anxious. The answer was not the medication but getting in the game and learning the antidote to apathy. Hundred dollar pharmacy bills became the money used for new experiences.

In finding the answer to their problems, my purpose was fulfilled. I was living the life I imagined. I have found purpose in helping others find their destiny. I share the joy of medicine, helping people learn to live the life they imagined.

— Scott Conard, MD

Embrace Silence
Dr. Wayne Dyer

You live in a noisy world, constantly bombarded with loud music, sirens, construction equipment, jet airplanes, rumbling trucks, leaf blowers, lawn mowers and tree cutters. These manmade, unnatural sounds invade your sense and keep silence at bay.

In fact, you've been raised in a culture that not only eschews silence, but is terrified of it. The car radio must always be on, and any pause in conversation is a moment of embarrassment that most people quickly fill with chatter. For many, being alone in silence is pure torture.

The famous scientist Blaise Pascal observed, "All man's miseries derive from not being able to sit quietly in a room alone."

With practice, you can become aware that there's a momentary silence in the space between your thoughts. In this silent space, you'll find the peace that you crave in your daily life. You'll never know that peace if you have no spaces between your thoughts.

The average person is said to have 60,000 separate thoughts daily. With so many thoughts, there are almost no gaps. If you could reduce that number by half, you would open up an entire world of possibilities for yourself. For it is when you merge in the silence, and become one with it, that you reconnect to your source and know the peacefulness that some call God. It is stated beautifully in Psalms, "Be still and know that I am God." The key words are "still" and "know."

"Still" actually means "silence." Mother Teresa described the silence and its relationship to God by saying, "God is the friend of Silence. See how nature (trees, grass) grows in silence; see the stars, the moon and the sun—how they move in silence. We need silence to be able to touch souls." This includes your soul.

It's really the space between the notes that makes the music you enjoy so much. Without the spaces, all you would have is one continuous, noisy note. Everything that's created comes out of silence. Your thoughts emerge from the nothingness of silence. Your words come out of this void. Your very essence emerged from emptiness.

All creativity requires some stillness. Your sense of inner peace depends on spending some of your life energy in silence to recharge your batteries, remove tension and anxiety, thus reacquainting you with the joy of knowing God and feeling closer to all of humanity. Silence reduces fatigue and allows you to experience your own creative juices.

The second word in the Old Testament observation, "know," refers to making your personal and conscious contact with God. To know God is to banish doubt and become independent of others' definitions and descriptions of God. Instead, you have your own personal knowing. And, as Meville reminded us so poignantly, "God's one and only voice is silence."

— Dr. Wayne Dyer

Shazam! The Time is Now
Carolyn Cummings

W here has the time gone? It seems like yesterday that I was 40, thinking that was middle age. Now, at 60ish, I'm positive that this is middle age. I certainly have a different frame of mind and revised viewpoint of what is really important in life.

I'm not sure exactly when "old cogger-hood" arrived. Maybe it was while shopping with my hubby, a young store clerk whispered to another store clerk, "Wow, look at those two old coggers." However, there really is a lot to be said for "old cogger-hood," like knowing how to better handle major happenings in life with action or when to just "go with the flow." (I have a better percentage of success nowadays.) It takes maturity to find out we are really in the driver's seat; it takes courage and passion to drive.

Gifts and Riches No One Can Buy:

Health: Even billionaires can't buy it, and no one can maintain it for us. We have found the essential oils and health alternatives are the best route for us. Keeping your personal vehicle in tip-top shape is a must as we can not get another one issued to us; I've asked.

Children's hugs: Children are truly the most wonderful, exciting gifts of life. They are so honest about who they love and who they do not. Their warmth and smiles can melt and mend even the toughest of hearts. Of course, grandchildren are our bonus for raising our own.

Laughter: It mends hearts, feelings, and emotions.

Animals (especially dogs): adoring looks, even without treats in your hand

Diamonds dancing on new fallen snow, rainbows and rain falling to sprout the flowers

A Gift to give to others in your life: Life Histories. Have relatives or special ones record their lives. They have lived through things we haven't. Write your own history because times are changing at the speed of light. As I look at the faded 100 year-old photos of my grandparents, I long to hear stories of the sod house, the challenges, the survival, the successes, the heartaches and the joys. At the turn of the century, they homesteaded a flat section of land in the corner of Oklahoma and Texas and raised 7 children, including my mother.

After Life Guarantee: Keep your "forever policy" using the "owners' operational manual" issued 2000 years ago. Reservations, I'm told, are being taken for long desired vacation spots. All the hubbub in the paper, TV and some violent movies are distracting at times, as well as the fighting over whose religion is the right one. As I remember, most religions have the same basic message: "Keep in touch with the Almighty; do good; love yourself and others, and certainly, 'stay outta trouble!'"

Joy: No matter what age we are, we make our own peace and happiness. Put negative folks on your "inactive list" and the grumpy ones on the "drop dead list." That old saying, "You are what you think you are," is so true.

Life now truly is a great adventure. As for us, we try to live up to the sign hanging by the front door: "Sunshine and Happiness Spoken Here."

— Carolyn Cummings

101 Goals

Mark Victor Hansen

Setting goals is one of the most important things you can do to guarantee your personal, professional and financial success. Goals are like a road map to your target destination. Each goal accomplished is another mile behind you on the road to your desire objective.

Most of us set goals in one form or another. But most of the time, we do not ask for enough, "I want to have a great job; I want my marriage to be successful; I want to have a million dollars."

These are goals for those who dip a toe into what they really want, but they are afraid to jump into the water. It is time to stop tip-toeing around the pool and jump into the deep-end head-first. It is time to think big, want more and achieve it all!

One of my favorite life-changing assignments is to have people write down 101 goals for themselves. This helps create a solid list of what they want to achieve in their lifetime. Then, after the initial list has been written, I ask them to create 10 outrageous goals by adding to their initial goals. These are things so extraordinary that 10 goals are all they need.

Why should people have 10 crazy goals? In order to come up with 10 outrageous goals, you must think outrageously. You must expand your mind and your realm of what is possible.

The bigger you think, the bigger your world becomes. You begin to think outside of yourself. The more you think outside of yourself, the more you begin to think and do for others. The more you do for others, the more rewards and benefits come back to you. It is a cycle that works for the betterment of both you and the world.

I believe, "Big goals get big results. No goals get no results or someone else's results."

— Mark Victor Hansen

The DNA of Success
By Jack M. Zufelt

M ark Twain identified a problem that is the crux of why people don't succeed. He said, "I can show anybody how to get what they want out of life. The problem is I can't find anybody who can tell me what they want." Earl Nightingale confirmed when he said, "Today in America people can become whatever they want. Trouble is most don't know what they want."

People try all kinds of things hoping they will find the magic bullet to make them successful. My research proves that goal setting, daily affirmations, visualization, positive thinking, motivational speakers and self-help gurus tell people to do things that just don't work. They promise to lead you to the promised land. The promised oasis ends up being a mirage.

A simple method exists for achieving success. Even though it is important, it is regularly overlooked. This critical ingredient is not based on what countless experts have been teaching. They serve up the same old philosophies based on goal setting, doing daily affirmations or visualization.

To achieve success in any area of life, a vital ingredient must be there. It is the catalyst for all success. Before I tell you what that ingredient is, I want to dispel two myths.

Myth #1 Goal setting creates success. The reigning king of all success techniques is goal setting. We've been taught that if we will write down our goals we'll be successful. And if we don't, we won't. My research shows that 7 or 8 out of 10 things a person writes on a goal list never happen. Everyone has many goals they didn't finish and many they didn't even start. Besides, we accomplish many things everyday that weren't written down on paper. In fact, you feel like a failure when you don't accomplish the things you wrote down.

Myth #2   Motivational speakers change lives. How long did you stay motivated after hearing a great speaker? Most people say, "two days," "two weeks," or "'till I got out of the parking lot." It's always a very short time. No matter how good they are, motivational speakers have no lasting affect.

What is this vital ingredient that must be present before success can be achieved? Where is the source of inner strength and self-motivation that keeps one hanging in there, persisting, constantly learning truths and being determined to make the necessary character and personality changes required for the level of success you want?

All these things come from one thing. Core Desires. A Core Desire is something you want with all your heart. Half hearted in anything doesn't cut it. When you identify a Core Desire it automatically unleashes what I call the Conquering Force that is within all of us. This Conquering Force causes us to have the discipline and ability to overcome all obstacles in our way.

Most people don't know how to identify what they want with all their heart. Desire is, indeed, the most important ingredient for success. It must be a genuine longing. An old Welsh proverb states that, "The hand will not reach for what the heart does not long for."

The journey towards your Core Desires will be enjoyable and full of enthusiasm no matter how difficult it is. The DNA of Success proves that success is, indeed, within our genes – and everybody has those genes.

Rudyard Kipling, Nobel Prize winning author said, it this way: "If you do not get what you want it is a sign that you did not seriously want it."

Identifying your Core Desires always causes success. That is a fact of life you can take to the bank. Success is not "out there" in some technique. It is an "inside job." So, how bad do you really want success in something -- with all your heart? If not, don't start down that path, for if you do you are destined to experience failure. If it is something you want with all your heart success is only a matter of time.

— Jack M. Zufelt

Live Your Highest Potential and Follow Your Bliss
Susyn Timko

I was always someone who looked for satisfaction from the outside. I thought I would be happy and successful if I could get love from a man. My life was only about others making me happy rather than what I could do to make others happy.

Throughout my acting career, I would go from class to class searching for the "big break," but I was never happy with what I was doing. I was not looking inside of me.

After a man I loved dearly rejected me and the constant struggle with my acting career, I was forced to look inside myself to find the love I was so desperately seeking from the outside world.

As I looked inward, I started to heal my life through meditation, reading books and attending seminars; I learned to love myself and give myself the love I was looking for from others.

I learned my reality was created from the way I talk to myself. By using positive affirmations, my life began to change. (An affirmation is any statement or belief that you repeatedly tell yourself such as "I can, I can" or "I can't, I can't.") These phrases are both affirmations; one is unempowering and the other is empowering.

I am now using empowering affirmations, and I am in love with myself. I no longer look for love and satisfaction through others. It is a miracle for me to be where I am today.

Through this inner journey, I surrendered to my life's mission, making a difference in the lives of children around the world. I am using positive music, books and videos to teach children how to love themselves.

Knowing children love music and how they listen to songs over and over again, I thought what better way for them to learn how special they are than through music.

I started a company that creates and produces positive products for children. All the songs are filled with the message of love. I designed the CD's with affirmations between each song, so children are always hearing how loved and special they are.

Not all of us grow up in a loving, supportive family. This music is for children from great families and those going through tough situations. I received a special thank you from an aunt of two small children. She explained the children are going through a tough situation and are not with their parents. She gave them one of my CDs, and they won't stop listening to it. It is their favorite CD. They know all of the words. Her nephew insists on holding the CD cover every night at bedtime as they sing along. This thank you moved me to tears.

I am so blessed to be doing this work for children and making a difference in their lives. Living my highest potential and devoting my life to children is an honor.

I surrendered to the Divine's plan by giving up the plan of how I thought my life should go. In doing so, I tapped into my natural talent of singing and songwriting that I didn't know I had. I believe that we all have at least one God given talent (gift). If we express it regularly, we would be in the flow of life instead of struggling. My mission is to help children to stay open to those gifts and to inspire adults to open up to the special gifts within themselves so we all can come out and play with our passions.

I am now open to the flow of life and loving it. My first CD, Loving Lullabies and More, is being sold in stores across America and on the Internet in over 50 countries. I am speaking and performing in schools, libraries, camps and bookstores. Many doors are opening for me, and I have no limits on where I can go and what I can do. I give this gift to everybody.

My advice for living your life's purpose and passion is to start to think like a child again. What was it that made you happy as a child? Did you like art? Did you like to sing? Did you like to help people?

Think about that; meditate on it. Look for the answers inside yourself. It may or may not take some time to discover your passions, but it is time well spent. After all, it is for you, and you are very important and worth the time. You are an amazing gift to the world.

May we all have a life of fun, passion, freedom and ease.

— Susyn Timko

Have You Ever Wondered What Your Life's Purpose Is?
Krystalya Marie'

Many of us live life trying to figure out our purpose. I say stop trying to figure out your purpose and live your life on purpose. If you do what you are passionate about, your purpose will become clear.

In 1997, after nearly a half century of emotional, verbal, physical and sexual abuse by multiple perpetrators, including myself, I was awakened to the fact that I had been sexually abused for most of my childhood. I had come to equate sex and abuse with love. After processing each event, I began forgiving my abuser knowing that I would grow and move beyond the abuse to a more joyful life.

In 2000, I finally faced the fact that I was still not completely healed. Though I had stopped drinking and my personal relation-ships were far more supportive, my workaholism was totally out of control, leaving little joy in my life. I realized that the abuse wouldn't stop until I began to completely love myself.

Part of the healing process included journaling. I found it helpful to ask and answer the following questions:

1. What brought me joy today?
2. How can I have more joy in my life?
3. Where are the lemons in my life?
4. How can I turn the lemons into lemonade?
5. What am I so entrenched in that I can't see beyond it?

I discovered that sharing insights about how to be empowered and to live life to its fullest potential brought me joy. I had been so caught up in the abuse cycle I couldn't see beyond it. The abuse was "my lemons," and teaching others to be self-empow-ered was the lemonade.

When I found a lump in one of my breasts the size of a golf ball in 2001, I was able to test out my belief by taking responsibility for my life. After a year of going from one holistic practitioner to the next, I began seeing and drawing healing symbols.

Shortly thereafter, I drew a symbol to remove the lump from my breast. Using this symbol, along with processes for emotional healing, the lump quickly disappeared. Since then I have drawn over 215 of these symbols and have developed simple processes for healing emotional and physical ailments.

What I came to realize is that every day of our lives we are living our purpose. Instead of focusing on your purpose, I recommend that you focus on what brings joy into your life, what you are passionate about and what gifts you have to offer others.

The following gems have helped me to live my life with passion and joy, my hope is that they do the same for you.

• Write in a journal at least 15 minutes per day, asking questions, like those above.

• Look for the positive in everything and your life will be more positive.

• Before falling asleep, visualize doing more of what brings you joy.

• Look for ways to make lemonade with life's lemons.

• Take responsibility for everything that happens in your life and empower yourself to make things different.

• Help others solve their problems and your problems will go away.

• Share your gifts with as many people as possible.

• At the end of each day, write down five things for which you are grateful.

If you want more joy in your life, ask, "What brought me joy today?" Start doing more of that now!

Love, Light & Laughter,

— Krystalya Marie

...As Yourself
Serina L. Cox

I'd learned it in Sunday school all those years ago: "Love your neighbor as yourself." I believed I practiced it as well as anyone and better than some. It seemed like a simple thing to do, though some neighbors were easier to love than others. No one said it would, or should, be easy. We were just to do it. But the emphasis was always on the "love your neighbor" part, leaving free the assumption that everyone had a perfect understanding of the "as yourself part. It was many years before I began to question the latter portion of this famous quote and its true meaning, but the journey led me to those questions. The answers helped me to grow in love and acceptance.

Corporate America was good to me. As a mid level manager in an enormous financial machine, I found the financial rewards to be gratifying. I was being good to myself, but something was missing from my life. My situation began to focus one day when a friend at work jokingly said to me, "You don't drink; you don't smoke, and you don't swear. Are you sure you belong here?"

I didn't feel that I belonged there. For the first time in my life, I had a position of responsibility and a sense of accomplishment. Yet, my physical health was in decline. I was in my late forties and considered some of the effects of the 'maturing process,' but the future of my comfort level in my own body didn't hold much promise for improvement which was due to stress. With my usual propensity to throw myself headlong into any endeavor, I set out to conquer stress.

My conquest of stress led me to Bill Harris and the Centerpointe Research Institute. His tapes suggested, among other things, yoga. Having already tried it, I was somewhat skeptical. But, I tried it again, this time using a form of yoga, which took my maturing body into account.

I fell in love with yoga. I became enthralled with the practice and decided that I wanted to become a yoga teacher. Yes, I would become a yoga teacher, and, in five or ten years, I would begin to slowly transition from my safe little niche in corporate America to teaching/semi-retirement, so much for the best-laid plans.

Two years later everything changed. It was the 1990's and corporate buy-outs were daily news. Of course, we were assured in my company that no such changes were in our future, but indeed they were. As employees scrambled to find new positions within the re-organized company, I saw an opportunity that, while bold, felt right. I would accept a severance package and find out whether or not teaching yoga was right for me.

It was a match made in heaven! I threw myself into teaching with ardent fervor, quickly expanding my class schedule to several classes each week. Before long I was teaching in yoga studios, a couple of gyms, a hospital and a private school. It was blissful. I was working fewer hours and finding more time to tend my flowers and watch the squirrels frolic in my back yard. I could meet a friend for lunch now and then or catch an afternoon matinee. Life was good.

Unbeknownst to me, I was learning to love my body for the first time in my life. Not the love that says, "Oh, look in that mirror, aren't I just the most gorgeous thing ever!" But the kind that says, "Gee, my back hurts this morning, but not to worry, I know just what my body needs to feel better and I love myself enough to give my body the attention it needs." It was all about releasing and letting go of the tension that I had stored in my body throughout my life. Tension had built up in my body, and my life, from lack of deep tender personal love that encouraged me to respond to my own needs so I could have the energy and personal resources to reach out to others as well.

As I began to bring this tender-loving kindness into my own life, I began to notice a change in my attitude toward others. I was beginning to love my neighbor more as I loved myself more.

Could it really be that easy? Just love myself more and there would automatically be more love in the world?

Besides, I had taken great care of myself in my old corporate America days, getting up at 4:30 or 5 a.m. each morning, going faithfully to the gym, doing my aerobic work and lifting weights. Come rain or shine, sickness or health, I had ceaselessly pushed myself. Was this love or merely discipline? What was the essence of loving myself? And then it dawned on me, it was what I saw in the eyes of the people who came to my yoga classes as they were leaving. Something was happening to them in the class that allowed that sparkle to come into their eyes. They were learning to love themselves more by simply doing a few yoga poses for an hour. By releasing the tension in their muscles, the tension in their lives began to find a healthier perspective as well. They were letting go of tight bodies and finding healthy lives. They were relaxing.

It seemed so simple, and yet being able to focus your attention on your own body long enough to find relaxation can be more of a challenge than many people are easily capable of mastering. I began to wonder how I could help them find relaxation when not in class. As I pondered this simple question, I found the answer standing in front of me one day in the form of one of my students saying, "I own a recording studio and I think you have a very soothing voice, have you ever thought of making any recordings?"

Well, I might have thought about it, but I never thought about it seriously, and yet here was opportunity knocking on my door. After a couple of conversations about the possibilities, an agreement was reached, and I began preparing to record my first relaxation CD, *Serenity, Guided Relaxation with Serina Cox*. As I read the reviews, I was heartened by the positive response from those lives I had touched.

I continue to be amazed at the way mature bodies accept and respond to the gentle nurturing of a tender and loving yoga class.

— Serina Cox

The Power of a Healthy Body
Maria Leslawski

The most important, basic requirement of every individual is to achieve and maintain good health. Your healthy body and mind will give you the power to succeed in that for which you have a passion and desire. The responsibility for your health, both mind and body, is yours alone. The body is your engine and you need to give it the right fuel – love, care and attention – to maintain it in good working condition.

The body's ability to operate relies on many factors, including a basic diet, the right nutritional supplementation and exercise which is moderate and consistent. The effects of stress are the cause of many degenerative diseases. Environmental toxins and drug use have, and continue to be, major health issues. An unhealthy lifestyle will cause break-down and disease.

Often we are so busy traveling the road of wealth that the last concern is for our health. We only have one body in this lifetime, and it deserves good health.

What is the point of wealth if we don't have good health to enjoy the fruits of our success?

The other day I met a business acquaintance who introduced me to a successful 84 year-old, retired business man – retired because his body had sent him the message that his stress level had to be reduced. He had striven to be successful and wealthy all of his life but had given no thought to his health. He was now pondering what success had meant to him and who would remember his success. His reevaluation and desire for a stress-free life came after two bypass surgeries. On the way home, I thought, "How sad that even though he realized he had ignored his well-being all these years, he was not prepared to take the extra step to find out what he could still do to improve his health."

He reminded me of another patient; he had a heart of gold but ignored his health. His wife and I sat by his bedside in intensive care as he slipped into a coma and died. His wife and I went to a separate room and spoke of the good times. I left when the family arrived and, seeing them support each other, thought to myself, "If only he had taken better care of his health." He was still a young man in his fifties who could have continued to live a good life.

I have a dear friend who has been an inspiration whenever times are difficult. With strength and determination, she has survived the roller coaster of life. From the time she was a young girl involved in the family business, it was work and study. She worked hard, achieved success, wealth and helped many others to succeed. Circumstances beyond her control forced the loss of success and money. Her health reached rock bottom, and she was at the pearly gates on more than one occasion. She drew on inner power to hold on and begin the long, slow path to recovery. The recovery is still in progress, and it will take time. The journey to success and wealth will also be achieved in time and on her own merits. She continues to help others be successful and help them in their own hour of need; although no one would help her in hers.

Make it your goal to have and live a healthy lifestyle, and have the inner power to achieve your wealth.

Success will be yours when you help others be successful.

To your health, happiness, success and wealth.

— Maria Leslawski

Giving Your Way to Greater Success
Dr. Peter G. Fernandez

*A*s a youngster, I doubted Mom and Dad's advice, "The more you give in this world, the more you will receive in return." It's hard to see a return on taking out more garbage or getting a B instead of a C in a class.

Having traveled a bit farther along life's path, I have acquired a strong appreciation for this universal law of success. Following this law has produced many riches for me. The formula is simple: if you only give a little, you will only get a little back. If you give a lot, you will get a lot back. The law never fails.

As a practicing chiropractor, I built a large, all-referral practice following this "give more, receive more" law of success. I gave my patients more personal attention, more quality care and especially more instruction on how to care for themselves. The more I gave my patients, the more they showed appreciation by referring their friends and relatives to me. Eventually, I opened 12 offices in different states, and each office followed the "give more" rule of success.

Today, as a consultant and success coach, I teach my clients how to apply this universal law of success to maximize their patient satisfaction in order to build highly successful practices. When people apply this "give to get" formula, they automatically become more successful.

I hold none of my practice-building secrets back. I make a point of speaking with legislators and others who can provide valuable services for my profession, and in spite of a continuously full schedule, I always make time to give my clients a same day response to their requests.

In addition, I "give more" to my profession by speaking for free at various state associations and colleges. I have also written over 200 professional papers and 17 books, teaching doctors how to give more to their patients by better educating their patients on what they can do to help themselves. I have doctors and other consultants constantly asking me why I'm "giving away the store" – giving away the secrets I've worked so hard to discover over the past 40 years? You already know the answer to this. I am not cheating myself of anything but simply following the universal law of "the more you give, the more you get back." In doing so, my management firm grew to be the largest in the world and many now refer to me as the Donald Trump of chiropractic consultants.

I am now using this success formula for a different cause. I am currently writing a book, *Neck Pain, The Prevention Secrets of One Thousand Chiropractors*. I am using this book to help teach the public the secrets of caring for their own neck problems.

At this point, the reader may have a question, "What's in it for you?" Who knows? The formula always works. The more I can help people take care of their own neck problems; the more they will appreciate my profession by referring others. That is my objective. I can't lose. It's the rule that never fails. "Give to get." Try it you'll like it.

I have learned that we control how much or how little success we achieve. If you want more, give more.

— Dr. Peter G. Fernandez

Tranquila
Dr. Karin Wilking

*D*uring a sabbatical, I had the opportunity to live and work in Costa Rica. After my family and I arrived, I began to notice how everyone would say, "tranquila, tranquila" to me. This Spanish expression means to "relax and put things in perspective." At first, I thought that this was due to the cultural differences between my American "time is money" philosophy and the Costa Rican "pura vida" (this is the pure life) motto. However, after months of daily "tranquilas" from seemingly everyone, I decided to take notice.

I tried to relax and adopt a more laid back attitude, which caused me more stress, because "life was to be taken seriously." The harder I tried to be "tranquila," the more frustrated I became. I could not shake the somber survivor mode that had accompanied me since the age of 12 when I found myself abandoned and homeless. Even though a very loving and compassionate family later adopted me, I never let go of my tough survivor exterior. My emotional armor served me well in my twenties as I struggled through an abusive first marriage, an obsessive student-turned-stalker and the molestation of my 3 year-old daughter. Life for me was a place where trust was just one step away from betrayal, good works were rewarded with suspicion and love was a conduit for abuse. So asking me to be "tranquila" was like asking me to walk the plank. I just couldn't do it.

I had spent my whole life up to that point, racing from one heartache to another. Although I had little control over my adversities, I did have a choice in how I would react to them – how they affect my life. It was time to let go of my tough armor of distrust that blocked both the worst and best of life's offerings. It was time for me to have faith in my Heavenly Father, my family, my friends and myself. Taking this leap of faith helped me realize

I didn't have to weather life's storms alone; God and others who cared about me were on my side. It gave me the strength to finally walk the plank and become "tranquila."

After mustering enough faith to knock down the walls that had kept me from attaining all that life had to offer me, getting to "pura vida" became instinctive. I lived in one of the roughest and poorest neighborhoods in Costa Rica, nicknamed "Little Hell." But as I got to know my neighbors, and they welcomed me into their extremely modest homes, I marveled at how happy they were. They weren't frustrated with their lot in life but were joyful and thankful. As I watched my children's transition to living in a foreign country, I saw they were completely content with their soccer ball and broken scooter – never missing their other toys, video games or cable TV. Simple things bring so much joy to life. I began to appreciate, more than ever, my great second marriage, my two healthy beautiful children, my large support network of family and friends and my career that allows me to help others live the life they love.

I will be forever thankful to the generous and kind people of Costa Rica for opening their hearts and culture to me. These humble people taught me that my life's struggles were my tools for personal growth, and that I too must share what I have learned to empower others. Today, when I teach and speak to various groups, I challenge them to live life to its fullest, by discovering the power of being faithful, grateful and "tranquila".

Pura Vida!

— Karin Wilking

The Gift of Opportunity
Alice Inoue

*I*t is a gift to have the opportunity to write my story, and I've found when I open myself up to gifts, the opportunities keep coming. It is the opportunities that I've taken that contribute to living a life that I love. It can be the same for you – once you realize the gift of opportunity is there for you to take every single day.

My mother is a beautiful, wise Chinese woman. She grew up in extreme poverty and was 26 years younger than my father. My father was a mean-tempered but good-hearted merchant marine who never finished the sixth grade.

I first learned of seizing opportunity from my mother's story, which I heard many times. Her world was strictly about survival. She would sometimes go days without food. When she met my American father and he declared his love for her, she saw it as a huge opportunity knowing it was her only way out of a desperate life, despite the fact her family threatened to disown her. She saw the gift of opportunity, married my father and came to America.

After I was born, we moved to Taiwan where I soon learned to speak Chinese.

Through the years, the adults would always speak to me about 'ji whei,' meaning opportunities. "Alice, look for the 'ji whei;' don't pass up any 'ji whei,' and don't hesitate when a 'ji whei' presents itself." Following this advice has done so much for me on my journey of life.

What I grew up noticing about the Chinese culture was that once they identify an opportunity, they jump on it without hesitation, knowing that they lose out if they don't. Since Taiwan is so overpopulated, there's much competition. Hesitate, and someone will beat you to it, the way bridesmaids jump for the bride's bouquet at a wedding reception without fear or wavering in their purpose.

I took this advice and this way of looking at opportunity to heart, and it became my way of being as I left Taiwan to attend college in America. It is only now that I can look back over the past 25 years and realize it is seeing the gift of opportunity that has allowed me to live so happily and so fully.

I have never regretted an opportunity that I have taken. In retrospect, absolutely everything I've done has enhanced my experience of life on multiple levels. Not that it was all easy, but what it really did was open me up to the fullness of what life has to offer.

The universe provides opportunities daily, though it may not necessarily be a gift of money or a gift of being able to write in a book, but the "gift of opportunity." You only have to look to see opportunity in front of you every day of your life. Open yourself up to the journey of the experience, and you'll see all the gifts the universe offers you can be claimed as yours.

— Alice Inoue

My Life Journey has Molded My Life Purposes
Kwai Lan Chan-Cook

*T*he streams sounded just like the coins dropping into the rocks flowing down the mountain. Above us, the morning sun escaped the eclipse of the mountain and illuminated the spectacular view. Below, in the jungle, my father and I walked, isolated, but not discomfited, by the mist.

It was here, with the spectacular view of nature and amidst the snakes, spiders and blood-sucking insects that my father taught me how to sense, smell, feel the chi (life force energy) and listen to the environmental sounds, especially the water.

The lessons between us were to understand Feng Shui. Both of my parents wanted me to be equipped with this skill, and I spent a portion of my childhood in pursuit of this knowledge, passed down from generations of masters — a knowledge which has brought me luck.

A recent example of this fortune is my real estate properties. My broker asked me how I increased the value of my property by $100,000 in less then 6 months. I realign a house's energy with the environment to attract the positive flow of chi into the property. Then, I rent the property and someone else can enjoy the benefits of the energy.

Feng Shui can enhance health, wealth and relationship. I was dismissed from the hospital when the surgeon could not find the lump in my breast. The United Kingdom commissioned me to help design a town in Kent. A company hired my services and subsequently increased its sales revenue by 40 percent within three weeks.

In addition to personal successes, I have also taught others how to use Feng Shui. One of my clients won a house in California within a week of applying the Feng Shui tips. A young printer has become a movie star in the movies *Save The Last*

Dance and *Dahmer*. He won an Independent Spirit Award in the movie *Dahmer* as the best actor by applying my instruction for less than a year. His success has given him free time to travel the world. I helped a cruise line business increase in revenue while a number of businesses suffered from 9/11 and "SAH." A single mother has united with her love one again after 13 years of separation with the help of Feng Shui. In essence, Feng Shui can "bring sunshine and smile into people's lives."

My mission is to help people become financially free in the strong countries of the world. These people would then have the free time to help the people in poor countries to live a better quality of life. Hopefully this would bring peace to the world.

— Kwai Lan Chan Cook

Thunder Guts Inspires
Roger Jones

*T*hunder Guts' voice boomed out, "Stand to the right and keep quiet."
Thunder Guts repeated he command in an even louder voice.
"Stand to the right and keep quiet." None of us moved or spoke.
Thunder Guts was very intimidating. Never did I imagine the
impact he would have on my life.

I was 15 and remember getting ready to walk into math class.
Thunder Guts was the nickname we gave to our teacher because
his voice would boom so loud that the whole school could hear.
Thunder Guts was in his fifties, tall and thin with a black/grey
goatee beard. He was very strict.

I had learned the trick in his class – never make eye contact
with him! You were far more likely to be asked a question if you
caught his eye. For 45 minutes, I sat obediently, doing as I was
told. As I watched the clock on the wall tick, I looked forward to
my next class.

You see, the school was a secondary modern school in
Portsmouth, a naval port in the south of England. Most of
the teachers seemed to have a habit of setting very low
expectations. In some of our "careers" classes, we were told
several times that no one from our school goes to college. We
were told to look for local jobs, not the most encouraging
thought to plant in the minds of teenagers. As strict as
Thunder Guts was, his approach was different. He was passionate, not resigned.

I remember one class with Thunder Guts before a "careers"
trip. As the class came to an end his voice boomed out: "Why be
the plumber when you can be the plumber's boss? Why be the
seamstress when you can be the factory boss?"

At that moment, his words meant nothing to me. I was
just looking forward to the trip to the local dockyard to see
how I could get an electrician or plumbing apprenticeship.

The following week flew by, and at the end of our next math class, before we went off on our "careers" trip, Thunder Guts said, "If you aim for the moon, you will hit the ceiling. If you aim for the ceiling, you will fall flat on your face"

One evening as I was walking home after a "careers" trip, I started to think about what Thunder Guts had said. "If you aim for the moon, you will hit the ceiling. If you aim for the ceiling, you will fall flat on your face." Then I thought about what he had shouted the week before. "Why be the plumber when you can be the plumber's boss? Why be the seamstress when you can be the factory boss?"

Then I thought about what the careers teacher had told us, "No one goes to university from this school." I certainly knew that was true. Rumor had it that someone had gone to university about seven years ago.

As I walked along, my mind started to wonder. A thought suddenly flashed into my mind. Why don't I aim for the moon and go to college? I made this my objective over the coming three years and always replayed Thunder Guts' words in my mind when I felt my goal was unreachable. I achieved my goal three times over with BS, MSC, and MBA degrees. I still think of the frightening, exciting passion in Thunder Guts' words when I consider my dreams and aim just that little bit further.

Now if you aim for the stars…

— Roger Jones

Carpe Diem
Feranda Alves Schmelz

What is your big dream? What do you feel passionate about? What was the secret of all those famous people who succeeded and left great legacies behind?

It's not what you do, your status or money that make a difference. It is about believing in yourself enough to put your whole heart into doing what you love. It's about the focus of your passion. You can become a winner only as long as you do this and follow your purpose with passion.

Do what it takes to be a winner. Take a decision; define what your purpose and passion is. Don't let anyone stop or influence you. It's your life – your only life – so take control of it. Otherwise, someone else will.

We all have passion and purpose. Have you found yours? If not, then you are not doing what you truly love. Many people study in a certain field because it runs in their family. For others, certain influences – perhaps certain people – made decisions for them. How do you expect to reach your ultimate goals this way? You need to focus on what you truly want, and then you will bloom like a beautiful flower.

The difference in people's success boils down to whether they have found their passionate purpose and if it is their focus. Your reality is the result of your focus, your attitude and your choices (thoughts, words and actions).

If you do what you love, you will feel an excitement and enthusiasm, and it will be a lot of fun. Are you one of those people who rather wish that they were doing something else? What would it take for you to live a fulfilled and happy life?

Take your decision today; don't wait any longer. It's up to you. It exists deep inside all of us and wants to be set free.

We all have the drive to be successful, to fulfil our mission, to realize our dreams. It's like a burning desire, an inexplicable strength and force within each of us. Stop for a moment; make a decision to find your purpose. What is it, how are you going to get there, and when? Write it down; visualize it, and live as if it has come true. Sooner or later it will. Do it with desire, and you will live a life filled with passion. You will experience the greatest accomplishment by living the life you love.

Stop preparing for the future; rather, enjoy the present. We all seem to be preparing for retirement.. What for? To look back and say what most people say, "I should have lived?" No matter how much we have, it never seems to be enough. It is not the quantity that counts; it's the quality of your life that truly matters.

Live your life – each moment – with magic. As the poet challenges us, "Carpe diem." You will discover endless happiness along with your true inner being. This way you will give and get the most out of life. Do what you love, and the rest will follow.

The purpose at this moment is to take action. Don't wait until tomorrow. We are all capable of contributing to a better world. It is essential for us to live our life to its full potential.

No matter who you are, what you do or where you come from, you are ready to begin. Have faith. Believe in yourself, focus and take the first step today! You do have a purpose in life. Take control of it and enjoy your journey.

— Fernanda Alves Schmelz

Finding Your Life's Passion

Are you possessed by a God?
Matthias Schmelz

"**E**nthousiazein" is Greek and means "possessed by a god." I strongly believe that the greatness of God is hidden inside of every living being, particularly human beings.

Nature is so full of wonder, wisdom, miracles and stunning beauty that we look at it with love, respect and admiration. In the past, humans protected nature only if it was to their benefit. We differentiated between useful, useless and harmful animals and plants – depending on whether they could be exploited (cows, sheep, chickens, etc.) or whether they "stole" from us (wolves, foxes, eagles, etc.). We protected the useful, ignored the useless and killed the predators. We actually managed to eliminate many species totally and irretrievably.

Today we acknowledge the worth of every animal and plant. We finally recognize the unique value of each species and its right to exist. Even snakes, scorpions and tarantulas are entitled to live and are protected by law. Nature does not have to perform any more in order to be preserved. It is only recently when we gave up our arrogant belief that we were God's only children and that every other living creature existed in order to serve us.

Eventually, we accept the responsibility for ourselves and for the environment in which we live. We recognize that everything on earth reflects the spirit of superior creation, and we admit that it is not up to us to decide about who may live and who must die. We humbly acknowledge that the planet we live on was not given to us by our parents but lent to us by our children. Every tree, every leaf, every snail and every fish represents a unique expression of the miracle called life and deserves to be appreciated, admired, adored, thanked for and preserved.

If we respect nature, how much more must we respect ourselves? Aren't we nature's most noble, most brilliant and most conscious results? Aren't we the great-grandchildren of the homo-sapiens who not only managed to survive in nature but who started to shape nature according to his needs? We still have his instincts. We still know how to hunt, how to hide and how to fight. Within a couple of minutes of evolutionary history, we turned into masters of our environment. We have been able to change the world more than any other species. Even the mighty dinosaurs disappeared leaving hardly any trace. Did they die out because they were not able to adapt to a changing world?

Humans have the extraordinary ability to adapt to almost any circumstance. We live on top of mountains as well as underneath the sea. We survive in the desert and we build homes out of snow. We eat fish, meat, grains and fruit. We even create new and very different forms of life. Genetic engineering enables us to eliminate inherited defects. Technology can manipulate plants, animals and the human race. We are following fast in the footsteps of our Father. Are we turning into gods?

I believe that we have always been miniature gods – tiny creators, imaginative ants. Deepak Chopra claims that we are thoughts that have learned to create the physical machine. Didn't we always imagine first and then create? Didn't we always believe before we saw?

If God is our Father (or Mother), shouldn't He or She be proud to watch His or Her children succeed? Aren't we proud when our children do what we taught them to do? The Bible says that God created us according to His image.

Eden Phillpotts wrote that the universe is full of magical things, patiently waiting for our wits to grow sharper. I believe that we just have to keep learning and growing to become who we were meant to be.

— Mattias Schmelz

Passionate Consciousness
Bill Harris

*U*p until about ago 40, I was definitely not living the life I loved. I was chronically angry, often depressed, and had one abysmal relationship after another, most ending in intense heartache. I had no real career and no idea how to create one. The direction of my life was down – at best, sideways.

This was all a blessing in disguise, though, because it created an intense motivation to learn what happy, peaceful, and successful were doing that I wasn't.

Today, I'm married to a wonderful woman who really loves me. I make ten times what I used to fantasize about in my wildest financial dreams. And, I have a challenging career dong something I love.

What's more, my anger problem is gone--and I haven't been depressed for even one minute in nearly fifteen years.

Now, at age 54, I truly am living the life I love.

This transformation happened because I discovered a few key principles that created tremendous positive change for me. They will work for you, too.

What are these secrets?

First, happy people acknowledge that they are creating their reality, internally and externally. They see circumstances as an influence, but know that what they do inside creates how they feel and behave, and what people and situations they draw to themselves.

For most people, this processing of external circumstances happens unconsciously--out of awareness. This makes it seem as if circumstances cause your feelings and behavior and what you attract into your life. When this happens, it seems as if you are at the effect of external causes over which you have no control. You feel like a puppet. When things are good, you feel good. When they're bad, you feel bad.

Happy people, however, even if they can't see how they're creating what is happening, know that they are. They take responsibility.

Another characteristic of happy people is that they act because of the possibilities they see. Where the unhappy person sees what is necessary, or impossible, the happy person sees what is possible. And, by focusing on what is possible, happy people make those possibilities come true.

A third characteristic of happy, successful people: they focus their mind on what they want and keep their mind off of what they do not want.

Here's what I mean by focus. When you think, you make what psychologists call internal representations: pictures, sounds, feelings, smells, tastes, or internal dialog. When you focus on something, you create an internal representation of it using one of these six thinking modalities

These internal representations can be of what you want...or of what you don't want. Take prosperity, for instance. You could focus on not being poor, or you could focus on being rich. That is, you could make a picture inside of poverty, wanting to move away from it, or you could create a picture of being wealthy, wanting to move toward it.

In both cases the intention is the same, but your brain doesn't care about your intention. It just sees the literal content of the picture. When you focus on riches, it thinks you want riches, and motivates you to see opportunities, find resources, and take action to be rich. When you focus on not being poor, it sees a picture of being poor, and motivates you to see opportunities, find resources, and take action...to be poor.

Most people focus on what they want to avoid without realizing the consequences of doing so. When they get what they focused on, they assume they didn't focus hard enough and redouble their efforts. This creates even more of what they don't want, which creates more frustration.

The other penalty for focusing on what you don't want is that you feel bad. In fact, all bad feelings, and all negative outcomes, are the result of focusing on what you do not want.

Instead of unconsciously and automatically focusing on what you don't want, consciously and intentionally focus on what you do want. When you do this, you instantly begin to create it…and you instantly feel good.

The final characteristic: happy people are consciously aware. As a result, their brain is less likely run on automatic, creating internal states and internal outcomes they did not intent and do not want.

How do you become more consciously aware? Two ways. The first is meditation. Though traditional meditation is very beneficial, at Centerpointe Research Institute we use an audio technology called Holosync to create deep meditative states, literally at the push of a button. This greatly accelerates the meditation process, and allows you to create increased conscious awareness very quickly.

Second, investigate your own internal processes: your beliefs, values, ways of filtering information, strategies you use for decision making, motivation, and your other internal processes. Centerpointe's Life Principles Integration Process is a structured way of investigating and changing these internal processes, allowing you to take charge of how you create your internal and external results.

There is a price to pay to live the life you love. But paying it is a joyful enterprise, and once you pay it, you will benefit for the rest of your life. So realize that you create your reality, learn to focus your mind on what you want and keep it off of what you don't want, and increase your conscious awareness through meditation and self-inquiry.

The life you love is waiting for you!

— Bill Harris

Unique Magic
David Kendall

*T*he seed of my dream was planted in 1989 at the age of 21 while traveling the world – Europe and North Africa. But it was in Thailand where I met someone who impacted my life. I met a young man from Chicago who was a professional magician, and I instantly recognized that I wanted to be a magician.

I don't know exactly why because I had never been around the entertainment industry. Standing much less performing in front of people was about as far from my goals I could possibly imagine. But something called to me, and it would not shut up.

Years later during a detour, I found myself studying education at the University of Victoria, but my burning desire for magic had not subsided. A few years into the program, I knew teaching at least in the educational system was not going to cut it. Inspired by legendary motivational speaker Tony Robbins, I decided to stop wasting my time and pursue my dream of becoming a magician.

Since 1989, I had been practicing and fuelling this magical passion. By the time I gave up on teaching, I was ready to start working as a paid magician. I began with regular gigs in restaurants and pubs while I worked my way into higher paying private and corporate party work.

By 1995 I decided to travel the world with my magic and set off back to Southeast Asia. After spending some time traveling in Thailand and Nepal, I persuaded the Westin Stamford Hotel in Singapore to give me a gig performing in venues throughout the hotel.

Not long after, I moved onto Bali, Indonesia and began working with several 5-star resorts.

I moved onto Perth Australia to begin a whole new chapter in my life. My stay in Australia extended over five years. Not only did I reach heights of success with magic I had never dreamed, but I also met the love of my life and began a family.

A new vision evolved and lead our new family back to Canada for yet another new venture. I believe the key to an adventurous life is following your heart. If there is one short formula that has made my life unique, successful and fun, it is constantly asking myself what I want, listening to my heart for the answer and having the guts to follow through – even when it doesn't make a lot of sense.

I believe another key element to living the life you love is just looking around at what everyone else is doing and doing the opposite. This may sound strange, but just try it. You will see the magic in it.

We arrived in Canada in 2000, and I started a personal growth company, Magical Mind Enterprises Ltd. Being a focused individual, this business has turned out to be a financial success and is helping many people in their quest for personal and spiritual growth.

I feel energized and excited everyday knowing that the tools we provide for people are life changing. It's thrilling to know you are helping so many people and at the same time watching my own family grow and prosper and most importantly having the time to spend with my children.

A big part of our mission at Magical Mind Enterprises is helping people wake up and live the life they love and be free. Having freedom and autonomy is in my opinion the real magic of life.

Look after your health as without great health, energy and vitality, it is difficult to be free and enjoy life.

Be Magical.

— David Kendall

Giving (With A Passion)
John Hall

*T*he most profound discovery I've made about my life in this world is that it's not about me.

Life is not centered on my goals, my ambitions, my peace of mind, my plans, my money or my toys. I wasn't created to serve myself. And I will never find who I am or what my destiny is to be by looking in the mirror.

Real living is about giving to others. It is giving for the sake of giving, without regard for what may come in return. It is making the choice to give as a lifestyle – with a passion.

This perspective makes all the difference. Our search for meaning, our search for significance, our search for purpose finds focus when we choose to give to others.

Real giving isn't just about money. It's about giving ourselves – our knowledge, our wisdom, our talents, our time – investing in the lives of others. This lifestyle does not need to revolve around a legalistic system of plans and percentage calculations; rather, it revolves around simply looking at the needs of those with whom we come in contact and reaching out with what we have been given.

Giving is not necessarily an expensive thing. We are all wealthy in different ways, so giving can be as inexpensive as a smile, a sincere "thank you," a word of encouragement or saying, "How are you?" to a total stranger - and meaning it.

Each encounter throughout every day of our lives presents an opportunity to contribute something beneficial to the life of another person. Each encounter is unique and none are coincidental. Just as there are no unimportant people, there are also no unimportant encounters, thus no unimportant giving.

From this kind of giving comes a sense of mission in life – a sense of motivation that for each of us there is indeed a higher calling. And from motivation that for each of us there is indeed a higher calling. And from this comes a basis for all answers when we ask ourselves the big life questions such as who we are to be and what we are to do. From this, we derive a level of satisfaction that is unequalled by self-serving pursuits.

We soon learn that giving of ourselves in small ways prepares us for the privilege and the responsibility of giving in bigger ways – in ways that change the lives of other people. This is what will ultimately define who we are and what our legacy will be.

We find ourselves by giving to others – with a passion.

— John Hall

Why Am I Here?
Deepak Chopra
From an Interview with Dr. R. Winn Henderson

*T*he majority of people on earth are unfulfilled or unhappy because they do not have a purpose or a mission. As a part of the human species, we seek purpose and meaning; we laugh, and we are aware of our mortality (that one day we will die). This is what distinguishes us from other creatures. Laugher, mortality and purpose become three important, crucial questions. We search for meaning – a deep significance to life.

Why am I here? Why have I been placed on the earth? We've been placed on earth to make a difference in life itself and in others' lives. In order to make a difference, we must find what we are good at, like to do, and benefits others.

We all have a mission, and my mission in life is to understand and explore consciousness and its various expression and also to share that with anyone who's interested in doing the same. It boils down to understanding the mechanics of healing, the rule of love. I would say to put it very simply, my mission is to love, to heal, to serve and to begin the process of transforming both for myself and for those that I come in contact with.

As part of my mission, I founded The Chopra Center. My mission: to educate health professionals, patients and the general public on the connection between the relationship of mind, body, and spirit and healing. I teach people how to find their inner-self (most people have lost touch with theirs). When we find our inner-self, we find the wisdom that our bodies can be wonderful pharmacies – creating wonderful drugs – you name it, the human body can make it in the right dose, at the right time, for the right organ without side effects.

The body is a network of communication. Our thoughts influence everything that happens in our body. The problem is many people automatically assume, "All I have to do is think positively, and everything will be fine." Because many assume this, they become unnatural and pretend everything is okay.

One must go beyond that; one must experience silence. It is when one experiences silence healing energies become involved and a balance is created. Psalms 46:10 says, "Be still and know that I am God." When the body is silent, it knows how to repair itself.

Pursuing my mission gives me fulfillment. It makes me whole. It makes me feel that I will continue to do what I have been doing. If I had all the time and money in the world, this is I what I would choose to do. It gives me joy and a connection to the creative bar of the universe. I have realized that the pursuit of my goals is the progressive expansion of happiness.

Pursue your goals and find your happiness, wholeness, and balance in this world.

— Deepak Chopra, M.D.

The Long Haul
Ed Rust

*T*o prepare for the future we, as human beings, need a sense of history. This is how we learn; how we grow. Learning from the past enables us to focus on our purpose – driving our future.

From the beginning, everyone has enormous potential. It is a matter of life and what you do with the experiences you face.

When dealing with "learning experiences," we must look at the overview – the big picture. When facing an obstacle, it must be looked at with caution by asking these questions: Is it hard to overcome? Will it slow me down? Am I looking at the obstacle as a pessimist or optimist? Can I go around the obstacle like I would a mountain? Can I break it down into pieces? Is it really an obstacle at all?

If you read an obstacle the wrong way, that's okay. You can't be embarrassed about honestly saying, "Hey, I messed up." The most important thing to remember is you can't take yourself seriously, but you must take your responsibilities with all seriousness.

Experiences give us character. They make us who we are. I was lucky to have had a unique experience with State Farm. When I first began my career, my managers took time to mentor me by teaching me from their experiences. Their example taught me how to be a great boss – a great mentor. Three broad principles emerged: First, you may not execute your philosophy as well as you like, but you can voice your advice about the details. Second, you can be successful by surrounding yourself with the "best people for the job." Finally, you must let your employees do their jobs – let them run and develop their own experiences.

If you have advice about the details, be a coach asking the right questions in a non-threatening manner. Touch what is on people's minds and in their hearts. Give credit away; don't keep it for yourself. Let others know what a great job they are doing.

Be a teacher, a cheerleader – not a rule-giver or a jailer.

It is a great mistake to assume the world is the same today as it was 10 years ago. Do listen to your intuition about the "changing world," but don't forget to ask, "Am I reading the world correctly?"

To make the long haul of life, discover your passion. Be willing to be a student of this; then, be willing to be a teacher. Open your experiences to others. We all make the wrong turn somewhere is this crazy experience we call, "life." When teaching, don't forget to be a coach not a lecturer.

It is your purpose to help others find and keep their passions. Do it with understand; do it with your own passion.

— Ed Rust

Overcoming Negative Self-Talk
Patrick Phillips

My dad left my mom, my two brothers and me when I was 12 years old. He moved to Las Vegas with another woman and I never saw him again. Somehow, my dad never paid any child support, leaving my mom to work two jobs to put food on the table. I remember seeing her for an hour or so each day when she got home from working at a print shop. She would fix us a quick meal and rush out the door to sell tickets at a drive-in movie theater until midnight.

To justify his failure to provide for his family, my dad let us know that we would never rise above his social or economic status in life. And, since we grew up in one of the poorest areas of the city, I believed I was destined to remain poor and in debt for the rest of my life.

Until I was 45 years-old, I believed that lie. Everything I did in life was subconsciously designed to keep me in poverty. I never kept a job more than a couple of years, and I tried, unsuccessfully, a number of attempts at starting my own business. Every time I got close to success in anything, I would think to myself, "You will never be more successful than your dad was. You certainly can't rise above your social standing. You will always just survive and do not deserve to prosper." Of course, those were not the exact words that I heard in my head, but the idea that I could never be wealthy or successful was always there, hauntingly reminding me of what I learned from my dad.

My negative self-talk was reinforcing what my dad had planted in my young brain, in so many ways, "You will always be right where I am now: poor, unhappy, unfulfilled and a failure." I mean, after all, this was my father, not some stranger. He was the ultimate authority in my life. There is no way he could be lying. I thought.

Then, in 1994, I ran across a secret that changed my life. I literally went from poverty to wealth within a couple of years. I found my passion.

I built a financial services company that generated over ten million dollars a year, with over 1,200 affiliate offices, nationwide. My wife and I moved out of our tiny 17-year-old home and built a new executive home in an exclusive neighborhood in northern Fort Worth. We started driving luxury automobiles, traveled all over the world and began to help family and friends in ways we could never have imagined a few years earlier.

The secret to my new-found prosperity was learning how to reprogram my brain for success and financial freedom. Changing the way I talked to myself was the key to overcoming all the negative input I had received throughout my childhood, and that I had unwittingly reinforced throughout my adult life. Finding freedom, I am able to live my passion – helping others.

I now give seminars and have written a book to help other people change their lives as I did through reprogramming their brains for success and financial freedom. Whatever you do, don't give in to the voices inside your head that may be holding you back. You can have everything you wish for in life if you just replace the old programming with new programs. As Napoleon Hill once said, "You are searching for the magic key that will unlock the door to the source of power; and yet you have the key in your own hands, and you may make use of it the moment you learn to control your thoughts."

— Patrick Phillips

HAVING A PASSION for the MASTERY OF LOVING!
Matthew G. Sikh II

I became a personal and family dynamics consultant and the developer of the "Mastery of Loving" Relationship Course due to my own personal life experiences. The trials and challenges in my life have fueled my desire and passion to help others in creating lasting and loving relationships in their lives.

Dr. Robert Schuller, a gifted man who is called "Minister of the Good News of Jesus Christ," says, "With God you can turn your scars into stars!" Looking back, I can see clearly how our Creator has orchestrated people and events to lead me through trials and challenges to my passion and purpose.

Growing up, I realized my parents, however well-intentioned in their own minds and hearts, fell short of understanding and providing for my own individual needs, as a child, to receive love in a meaningful fashion. At the age of 12, a spiritual experience led me to know deeply and completely Jesus' personal message to love one another.

My brother Mike was killed the day before Christmas Eve in 1970 while serving in Vietnam. We were extremely close, and I loved him very much. In my extreme hurt, I chose to be angry at our Creator and turned away from Him. Through this time in my life, I did keep the personal message of love toward others (that His Son gave me) alive in my heart. Little did I realize then that our Creator kept loving me even though I had chosen not to love Him.

The result came in 1988 when my daughter, who is extremely special to me, was born. Participating completely in the creation of a life was wonderful, spiritual, and powerful; it made me realize the awesome presence of a Creator of all life. I assisted in delivering my daughter in a water birth. She came out of her mother's womb into my very hands! Being a father to this tiny infant and watching her grow drew me closer to understanding there was indeed a Father of all of us, and there are natural ways that we can be safe and secure in His hands!

He began to reveal to me how He would use and direct me to help enhance and restore marriages, to bring more joy, peace and love into anyone's relationships, whether they are single, parents, children, friends, co-workers or even strangers. I became very serious and passionate about this work that our Creator had called me to because of the enormous need in today's society. In the last two years, I have been directed by Him to expand The "Mastery of Loving" Relationship Course on a national and international basis. I once asked Him, "Why did You choose me?" At the time, I was going through a "Moses" experience – feeling uneasy about being called to publicly bring this information to the masses. He answered, "Because you listened, and you cared."

"The Mastery of Loving" Program is now available to those who desire a unique and complete understanding and practicality of how we can love ourselves and others more, and on purpose. We are translating the program into other languages to help even more people.

Romans 8:28 says, "We know that in everything God works for good with those who love him, who are called according to his purpose." This fuels the passion everyday in my life!

— Matthew Sikh

Graduating From Personal Growth
Ron Wypkema

*I*n the spring of 2002, my life changed forever. I had a profound shift in consciousness.

I should have been free from stress and anxiety. After all, in 1980, I began intensive personal growth through meditation and spiritual exploration. Then, in 1984, I started a private practice coaching people on how to live in the moment by getting free of psychological and emotional issues. By 1987, I was leading workshops internationally.

Still, I was puzzled, why after decades of personal growth, I was still working on myself. Despite knowing and teaching that now is all there is, I was still identifying with the mind and emotions.

On that day in 2002, it occurred to me that there must be a better way to get free of the problems of the self. I put aside all of my learning and emptied my mind. Suddenly, I had a flash of insight about how to dis-identify from memories and the emotions associated with them.

I immediately applied this insight to a memory that had been troubling me. Instantly, all of the negative emotions about that memory effortlessly vanished. There was a profound shift in consciousness. One moment, I was myself dealing with an emotional issue; the next, the self I had identified with my whole life disappeared like a puff of smoke in the morning breeze. There was pure awareness, oneness with all that is.

All of the problems, worries and concerns of the mind had vanished. Instead of the noisy mind, there was utter silence, serenity and joy. The now was so full; all ideas of past and future had dissolved. This eternal timelessness was freedom itself.

At some point, the mind came back. I chose another emotionally charged memory to work with. This memory was the last time I had seen my 86 year old father alive. I applied this new awareness technique to this second memory. Again the emotions dissolved into the pure peacefulness of the moment.

As a result of being able to easily access this state of universal clarity, a complete system of awareness methods for freedom from the self and it's problems have come to me. Since it has come from the now and opens people to the now (the state of oneness), I call the work The Now Process™.

I share the methods of The Now Process™ with people around the world. I teach people how to graduate from being a seeker on the path of personal growth. My life work is about Turning Seekers into Finders.™ Many tell me that in a brief phone session, they have received more transformation than they had in years of working on certain issues.

For over 20 years, I had been devoted to personal growth. The astonishing insight that came to me that day in 2002 helped me to recognize that personal growth work is working on symptoms not the problem! Amazingly, I did not have to fix myself, improve myself or get rid of any of the remaining negative emotions I had, in order for this profound liberation of oneness to occur. All the personal growth work I had done was based on a false premise, there is a separate self. Now it was clear why I was still stuck in the mind, dealing with "issues." Personal growth itself could not lead to freedom. Why? Because, despite having the best of intentions when we do personal growth, it perpetuates the myth of separation. It perpetuates the illusion of a separate self.

Regardless of whether a person is a beginner at personal growth, or has been on the path for 20 or more years, it is possible to become free right now.

The true being is freedom, peacefulness, oneness, wholeness and completeness. The true being is love itself, eternal, pure awareness and universal intelligence.

Waking up to this universal oneness is possible in this moment. You don't need to improve yourself for years before it is possible to wake up to this reality. No time is required, since it is already here.

Until we wake up, the joke's on us, and no other joke has so much potential for creating so much suffering. The ego self is fiction. The "I" is the only real problem.

It is such a blessing to be of service in helping people to wake up to the light of the true being. As our identification with the mind and ego diminish, the limitless expressions of true freedom and higher potential are easily discovered. This moment is the moment to retire from seeking. This moment is the moment to wake up to find your true birth right.

— Ron Wypkema

Never Burst a Bubble
Captain Gail Harris, USN (Ret.)

*I*f you have a dream, know this: your dream is a glimpse of your future. This is the major life lesson I have learned. If you stay the course, stay focused and pray, you will overcome all obstacles to achieve your dream.

The road that led to my career in Naval Intelligence is a living example of this. I grew up in a poor section of Newark, New Jersey called the Central Ward. When I was 5, I was watching a movie with my father called Wing and a Prayer starring Don Ameche. It was about the aircraft carrier USS Enterprise in the aftermath of Pearl Harbor and the days leading up to the Battle of Midway. Just before the climatic battle, there was a scene where Ameche's character, Commander Harper, was giving the pilots an intelligence briefing. It was a detailed rundown of the Japanese forces they were going against and the capabilities of that force. I turned to my Father and said, "Daddy, that's what I'm going to do when I grow up." My Father smiled and said, "Okay."

I was too young to know it then, but he was a man way ahead of his time. He could have killed my dream by explaining that the odds were against me. He had been in the Army when blacks were still segregated outfits. He told me he had been in the Army but when relating his experiences, he didn't dwell on the segregation and discrimination he'd experienced. He didn't tell me there were very few African-American male officers in the Navy, let alone females. He only encouraged me.

The Navy would not open most of its career field to African Americans until the early 1970's, and for women, not until the mid 1990's. In the case of women, there was actually a federal law that prohibited them from serving aboard any ship that might go into combat. In the early 1970s, the Navy did begin assigning women, in small numbers, to support ships such as supply and repair ships, but it was not until the law changed in 1994, in the aftermath of the Tailhook scandal, that significant numbers of women were allowed to go to sea.

Since most of the Navy's aviation squadrons operated aboard aircraft carriers it would seem that my dream was impossible; yet, in 1973 I became the first woman assigned to an operational aviation squadron as an intelligence officer and at the time of my retirement in December 2001, I was the highest ranking African American female in the Navy. I know that hindsight is 20/20, but in my mind there is no doubt that at the age of 5, God gave me a glimpse of my destiny. There is for me no other plausible explanation.

This dream was no mere passing fancy. From the time I saw that movie, I was completely dedicated to the Navy. Whenever I heard, "Anchors Aweigh" played in movies, I'd get up and start marching around the house. In school, I'd draw scenes of naval battles in my spare time. I always rooted for Navy in the annual Army/Navy football classic. Looking back, one would think this was all pretty weird, but my parents were always supportive and never made me feel that there was something wrong with my dream or it would be impossible to obtain. They always said this is America and you can be whatever you want when you grow up.

During my college years, my dream lay dormant on the back burner of my mind. Because of the turmoil surrounding the Vietnam War, service in the military was very unpopular. It was still something I wanted to do.

As graduation approached, I was uncertain of my next step. I had received a scholarship to a two-year graduate program at the University of Denver's School of International Studies. My family felt you should grab any educational opportunity that came your way. I was the first in my immediate family to go to college. I accepted it, but knew in my heart I was tired of studying history. I wanted to go out and start making it.

I wasn't a very good student. One of my academic advisors was Dr. Josef Korbel, Madeleine Albright's father. He took the time to call me into his office and ask me what was wrong. He felt I could be an outstanding student but wondered why I wasn't working to my full potential. I shared with him that I felt guilty because I had never quit anything before. After a lot of agonizing, I dropped out and joined the Navy.

The minute I moved toward my goal, obstacles fell by the way-side. At the time I applied to the Navy, they were only accepting one out of every five women. Not counting the Nurse Corp, the Navy only had 400 women officers and 4,000 enlisted women on active duty. Because of the legal restrictions, job opportunities were limited to careers in administrative fields. I told the recruiter I wanted to be an intelligence officer. She said it wasn't possible at the time but things were starting to change. I signed up even though it appeared my dream job was not available.

The title of the movie I had seen long ago was prophetic. I literally joined the Navy on a wing and a prayer. My faith was rewarded. At the time of my graduation from Officer Candidate School, the Navy had opened up its intelligence training to women. There was one opening for my class. I was chosen because of my one year in graduate school. Upon arrival at the school, I was told by the instructors because of federal law I would not be able to go to an aviation squadron. I countered by asking why I could not go to a land based aviation squadron. Since they always operated from a land versus sea based location, the federal law would not apply. I worked hard in school, and by the end of the course, the Navy decided to make me a test case for women in operational aviation squadrons. Against the odds and existing laws, I was able to live my childhood dream.

If I had any doubts about this being my destiny, they vanished. One day shortly after I retired, I reflected on a couple of coincidences I had never noticed before. My father had been born in Enterprise, Alabama. That was the name of the aircraft carrier from the movie I'd seen long ago. My mother had been born in Midway, Alabama. That was, of course, the name of the famous battle depicted in the movie.

Dreams really do come true.

— Captain Gail Harris, USN (Ret.)

Wake Up...Live the Life You Love,

Transform Your Fear Into Focus!
Waldo Waldman

Fear is the greatest deterrent to success. It drains our ambition and denies us power to overcome challenges we face personally and professionally. When we let fear control us, we are destined to fail. When we control our fear and channel that energy in productive ways, we succeed.

How do you handle fear? Does fear control you, or do you control your fear? Do you become overwhelmed and give up, or do you face it with courage?

As a combat decorated fighter pilot, with 65 missions in hostile territory, I had to face my fears every day: getting shot down, letting down my country and my wingmen and failing to accurately perform my mission responsibilities. If I wasn't able to handle this fear, I would have surely failed. I had to realize that I had the power to overcome fear.

The key to my success was in my ability to direct my focus towards three distinct areas. Obviously, we are all not fighter pilots flying combat missions; however, the same lessons of focus can be applied to everyday life. Here's how you can apply these fundamental principles for overcoming fear:

Focus on your mission – Accept responsibility for accomplishing your mission objectives and feel confident in your training and preparation. Why are you needed, and who is depending on you to get the job done? When you take the focus off of yourself and your fear, and direct it towards how your mission will positively impact the lives of others, you find purpose in life.

Focus on your wingmen – Who is on your team that you can trust to get the job done? Who are the trusted and reliable partners in your life? Who can you turn to for love, inspiration, advice and courage? Perhaps it is your spouse, best friend, business partner or co-worker. By focusing on all the wonderful, supporting relationships you have, you become more courageous and confident to tackle life's challenges. You don't have to fly through life solo, if you have faith and trust your wingmen!

Focus on winning – See the success you want in your imagination first. Remember, the body achieves what the mind has rehearsed. If your mind thinks failure, you are setting yourself up for failure. But if you train your thoughts to envision winning, if you imagine with perfect clarity overcoming your challenges with courage and achieving victory, then you are destined to win.

Finally, the most important part in handling fear is to embrace it. Accept your fear and learn from it. Don't fight it or attempt to eliminate it, as it is a battle that can never be won. By experiencing fear, we become more human. Fear teaches us that we are not perfect nor are we superior to anyone else. It makes us more compassionate as we realize the frailty of life and emphasizes what truly is important in our lives.

Regardless of where you are, when you transform your fear into focus – on your mission, your wingmen and on winning – you are sure to be victorious in all that you do.

Now, Focus your Energy, Accept Responsibility, and make it happen!

— Waldo Waldman

Abundance, Prosperity and Fun
Sandy Forster

*F*our years ago I was running my surf-wear design business and desperately wanted out. I was sick and tired of working seven days a week and fed up with not being able to do what I wanted, when I wanted. I was terrified of my $100,000 debt and going backwards – fast. To say I was fairly stressed would be a mammoth understatement.

I was tired, scared, frustrated, broke and unhappy. I was smiling on the outside but crumbling on the inside. Constant financial stress made me yell at my two beautiful children, I was what I call a "crummy mummy." My dreams were huge, but my life was so small. I had no idea what to do or how to get out of debt.

I listened to a tape that said, "There is magic between the pen and the mind." It suggested I write down my ideal day. It sounded like fun. I began writing, "Morning: meditate, practice yoga stretches, go for a run down the beach; dive into the ocean; get the kids to school and head to the gym. Afternoon: read some inspiring books; listen to personal development tapes; and share what I learn with others to make a difference in their lives."

Keep in mind, at this time I was in enormous debt and working a 7-day week in a business I didn't enjoy. I said to a friend, "If I was living my ideal day, I'd never have time to make any money."

The universe works in mysterious ways, and once I'd written "my ideal day," miraculous events began to unfold. Within five months, I was attending a training session for the new business I was building. We were told, "To be truly successful you should plan your day" and given a day-planner to complete for homework. That night back in my hotel room I began to think - how did I spend my time these days? Let's see, meditate, yoga, beach, gym, personal development.

Chills ran up and down my spine as I filled in the sheet. I remembered writing an identical list, months earlier, thinking it was impossible. Here I was living it and making over $100,000 a year! In that moment, tears of joy and gratitude came running down my face. I realized, not just in my head but in my heart, that I actually had the power to write the script for my life.

Four years later, I have a lifestyle many only dream of having: owning a beautiful home with a pool and a hot tub, driving a stylish car, travelling overseas when I fancy, and owning investment properties around the world. My passion is inspiring others to transform their lives through the secrets of abundance and prosperity. This is my true purpose, one that continues to fill me with excitement, gratitude and joy. I have studied and applied dozens of century old secrets and experienced the most incredible results. My life is so vastly different compared to that financially, emotionally and spiritually bankrupt single mom I used to be.

The best part of all is I spend my days doing what I want. I continue to study the metaphysical and prosperity. I attend all the personal development workshops, seminars and events I want. My children say, "You're a fun mum now!" I knew in my heart I was destined for more.

My belief is that you will experience more because the universe always has bigger and better plans for you. Whatever you may be experiencing in your life right now, you have the power within to create your future. The first step is get clear on what your ideal life looks like "write it down" and with the right mindset, mentors and motivation, you too can discover your purpose and live the life of your dreams!

— Sandy Forster

Sugar, Passion, and Happiness
Helen Shanley

As a child, I knew I walked in the sunlight of God's love. I was blessed at an early age.

I recognized all of the colors at six months and talked at eight months. I began walking at ten months and reading at two and a half. My advancement continued; I could say the Latin names of, and point to, the parts of the brain and the bones of the body and knew the capitals of all 48 states by three and a half. At the age of six, after reading the Old Testament stories and the entire New Testament, I asked to be baptized. I adapted a book into a play, which I directed, starred in, prompted and produced for the school assembly at seven. A semester before I was doing second-grade level hand work, third-grade level arithmetic, fourth-grade level geography, seventh-grade level spelling and eighth-grade level reading. No one was pushing my development. I loved my life.

When I turned 14, my world crashed around me. I have spent most of my life trying to put it back together. Along the way I did some writing, earned college degrees, developed a new way of teaching and took ministerial training, but I wasn't happy. I felt I had failed in so many ways. Because of this repeated feeling, I felt doomed to be always on the verge of success, only to fail. Yet, I knew from experience that happiness is the truth of life.

Recently, it occurred to me to ask for fulfillment as a way to overcome these feelings of failure and the sense of guilt that followed. I knew I needed to surrender to this fulfillment.

Now, at age 85, I'm living a life I love. I'm a licensed practitioner of religious science. I get to do everything I love: singing in the choir; being with people; praying for them and seeing their lives transformed; teaching Sunday School children individually that they can have what they want and how to help themselves; using depth imagery in transformational meditation services; getting speakers for my writer's club; facilitating both poetry and fiction groups and doing creative editing. I offered a simple exercise class in my neighborhood, and after 25 years people now greet me by name when I take my walks.

Sugar on My Lettuce, the first book in a three-part memoir, is being published. My stories and poems are broadcast over Valley Public Radio. The poems and stories I'm writing now are among the best I have ever done.

Even though much of this was going on before I asked for fulfillment, I wasn't happy. Now, I know the universe wants me to succeed. I'm not trying to accomplish anything, not pushing a stone up a hill. I'm allowing myself to be fulfilled.

Anyone can do this sort of turn-around. It's definitely worth it. And I'm worth it.

— Helen Shanley

Peanut Butter and Jelly

Jilliana Raymond

My oldest son was pursuing a biology degree and, if you are familiar with university scheduling, you know that degree programs are rarely completed on time. Near the end of his first senior semester, it was evident we would be funding an additional semester. As a single parent with two sons in college, our family was living on a strict budget and I was concerned by the added cost this extended stay implied. Luckily, I had time to request the necessary funding for the additional semester and wisely, I even allowed a three-month cushion to give him time to seek employment or pack his belongings before returning home.

Shortly after obtaining the extra semester's worth of funding, my industrious scholar informed me that he was enrolling in an ancillary curriculum that would require a fourth senior semester to complete. I was definitely not prepared to fund the added expense of this zealous surprise. My firm response was, "Get a job!"

Undaunted, my academic senior vowed to complete the program with or without the necessary funding. Upon further inquiry, I discovered he was studying life support classes sponsored by the campus rescue squad for which he volunteered. He then informed me it would be quite difficult for him to secure steady work, as his volunteer shifts would interfere with any routine employment. At this point, I considered the sanity of his rationale.

Two months later, I received a call from his very concerned girlfriend, asking if I was aware my son was surviving on peanut butter and jelly sandwiches. Concerned for his well being, I managed to forward very limited funds for food and again informed my industrious child to get a job.

With his courses completed, he returned home and immediately filed for employment with the fire department. While still not employed, it was becoming obvious he had a plan. He knew competition for entry into the fire academy was substantial. Thousands apply every year and only sixty earn the career of their dreams. Even if accepted, the six-month training would physically and mentally challenge his endurance beyond all his experiences.

Preparing for his goal during his two senior years led my son through a series of emergency care classes, where his passion for fire and rescue blossomed. He wanted to be a paramedic because he knew he could make a difference in people's lives. Charged by the knowledge that his biology degree, in combination with his advanced life support training, strongly enhanced his qualifications, and in spite of my funding concerns, my inspired son never lost sight of his future.

The nourishing ingredients in those jars of peanut butter and jelly consisted of one part goal, one part plan, two parts endurance and three parts perseverance. His plan, endurance and perseverance paid off. Today he is a paramedic and firefighter in one of the largest fire departments in the world.

His passion is saving lives.

— Jilliana Raymond

Intuition
Robin Barbero

*I*n 1974, when Rob Spears discovered the lymph glands under his arm had swollen to the size of a golf ball, he was anything but alternative. Within a week a biopsy led to the surgical removal of a tumor and a diagnosis of non-Hodgkin's lymphoma.

A rapid whirl of consultations with oncologists, motivated by a growing and paralyzing fear, led to one session of experimental chemotherapy, the toxic effect leaving him so desperately ill and devastatingly wretched for a week that he decided to forego any further sessions. Confronting his doctors, they finally admitted the treatment might buy him a few extra months but, in fact, had not proven to be successful as a cure in any of their trials.

With nothing to lose, he left the care of his doctors to pursue a path of self-discovery. He experimented with bio-feedback, hypnotism, meditation, cleansing, mega-vitamin and mineral therapies, making adjustments based on the results of hair analysis and blood tests.

He met a doctor, an internist turned psychiatrist, who had recently discovered many of his mentally disturbed and hospitalized patients had severe food allergies and chemical imbalances that led to their deteriorating mental condition. In some extreme cases, the simple removal of a food group was the difference between a normal life and hospitalization. Rob became convinced he should forget about the symptoms of his disease and concentrate on detoxifying and bringing his body into balance with organic foods and supplements while removing all allergic foods from his diet. The months turned into years and Rob was still among us, constantly adjusting his supplements and diet, growing healthier while pursuing wholeness on spiritual, mental and physical wholeness. There were set-backs, but each fall in his T-cell count, or descent into illness, taught him that he was in charge of his wellness, learning how his body responded to diet, stress and lifestyle.

Brenda Michaels was on a path of parallel discovery. In 1975, diagnosed with cancer of the cervix, doctors performed a hysterectomy. Given a clean bill of health, she, nevertheless, developed cancer in her left breast in 1988. After a full mastectomy, she was placed on Tamoxifin. She took Tamoxifin for four months but became so severely ill she stopped taking it. Her doctor was furious, but her intuition told her it was making her worse. Her doctor tried to convince her she was recovering, but Brenda knew something was amiss. Late in 1989, a mammogram revealed cancer in her right breast. After losing her second breast, both her surgeon and oncologist tried to convince her to go on chemotherapy. This time, despite the vehement objections of her doctors, including a pronouncement giving her only a year to live, she decided to follow her intuition and withdraw from their treatment.

Brenda soon discovered an herbalist and a holistic physician who started her on cleansing routines, mega-doses of vitamins, minerals, and herbs as well as organic foods. As she began to take charge of her healing, she also began looking at the emotional and spiritual components of her disease. Within months, Brenda began to have more energy, more clarity and a sense that her body was responding to the dietary, emotional and spiritual work she was doing. Her spiritual work included prayer and meditation; her emotional work was about discovering how she had suppressed her feelings and emotions over the years in order to please others and gain acceptance from those she loved. As time went on, she got healthier.

In her thirties, Robin Barbero was in excellent health and at the peak of her career when she was suddenly stricken with the Epstein-Barr virus/Chronic Fatigue Syndrome. Her symptoms ranged from excruciating headaches and nausea, to joint and muscle pain, night sweats, and shortness of breath. Within months she could hardly get out of bed and developed gastritis, gastroparesis and a spastic colon. The result of this was that she was left disabled and bedridden for over eighteen months.

She was living on a feeding tube, and her doctors were about to remove her stomach when one doctor suggested that her condition might be reversible. This physician knew that his therapies would only lead to a downward spiral, but he believed there were alternatives that might reverse her condition. That is when Robin began working with acupuncturists, energy healers, cranial-sacral massage therapists and nutritionists, starting to rebuild her immune system. She also began reading books by Dr. Bernie Seigel, Norman Cousins, Louise Hay and a roster of spiritual self-help advocates. Eventually she came to realize that living your life passionately and letting go of one's fear leads to a healthier body, mind and spirit. Courageously, she removed her feeding tube and, despite her doctor's prognosis, she discovered she could eat food again. She slowly introduced organic and nutritious foods into her diet and discovered she tolerated these foods very well. Ultimately, her health returned and she grew stronger.

Each life was changed forever. Each one learned that these diseases were gifts, bringing to them a level of consciousness and passion they had never experienced before. They discovered that healing is a holistic process with spiritual, emotional and physical components. You have to have hope, faith and the courage to face your emotional issues as well as the proper nutrition to feed your body. You develop hope and faith from a strong spiritual discipline such as prayer, meditation, yoga, breathing, etc. To develop emotional well-being, one must be willing to recognize wounded parts as the emotional precursors of disease and illness. Nutritional well-being is developed by giving the body what it needs.

— From Robin Barbero
Conscious Talk Radio Network May 11, 2004

Sustaining Higher Energy
Lake Furney

*H*ow can we live a life we love? We tell ourselves it must be found in some truth. If we are not currently experiencing a life we love, it must be a truth we haven't seen yet. Some people's experiences allow them to associate truth with happiness, while many more people experience a truth that life is cold, harsh and even cruel.

So why do people have such radically different perspectives and dramatically different experiences from one another? It is because energy creates perspective, perspective creates perception and perception creates experience.

Imagine a round diamond the size of the earth, with facets the size of counties on the surface. We'll call this planet "Truth." Standing in the middle of one of these facets, your perspective is limited to as far as you can see. You perceive Truth as a two-dimensional place. So, experience is a two-dimensional life if you never visit the boundaries of your individual facet of Truth. If you are adventurous, you might walk to the edge of your facet and see more facets of Truth that lie at slightly different perspectives. Each of these facets extends out as far as you can see. Your perspective is broader because you can see other facets of Truth, and your experience changes because you have perceived that Truth has more than one facet.

Now, imagine a ladder in the middle of your facet that goes straight up into the sky. We'll call this ladder "Energy." You climb a few rungs. Suddenly, you see that other facets of Truth surround you. The higher Energy you reach, the greater perspective you have, and the more facets of Truth you are able to perceive! Eventually, if you climb high enough, you see Truth as a multi-faceted, three-dimensional reality. If you can climb high enough, the facets disappear all together.

Does this all mean that we should just keep our heads in the clouds and ignore the problems we face on this planet? Absolutely not. Holding this higher perspective and energy brings love, kindness and peace to the troubles we face. It is only through a higher perspective and energy that we find any real solutions to our problems; the solutions that come from love and higher energy are fair and kind to all. As the magnificent Dr. Wayne Dyer put it, "We cannot get sad enough to help one person overcome sadness."

Likewise, we cannot get angry enough to settle one difference. We must bring love and joy to sadness and anger.

So, how can we find the energy that allows a higher perspective? Most of us understand the basic idea of how a radio works. We are constantly bombarded by radio waves that contain thousands of different frequencies. We turn the dial, and the inside of the radio "tunes to" the frequency of the music you want to hear.

Just like the radio, we can tune our mind in to the music of life we want to hear. It can be music of love, beauty, abundance and happiness (higher frequencies); or music of hate, ugliness, lack and unhappiness (lower frequencies).

The task then is to turn the dial to the right frequency. But most people's tuners are pre-programmed like the buttons on most stereos and car radios. We can learn to turn our dials to higher frequencies through the practice of meditation.

We are a system of energies. As you meditate, you achieve deeper brain waves that allow your mind to tune in to higher frequencies of energy. As you sustain this exposure, your energy system entrains to the higher energy all around and within you.

Sometimes, there are things that interfere with our reception. We may have a broken antenna, or the circuits inside our radio may be dirty. There are many resources to help us fix our "tuners," and many places to find the inspiration, resources, methods and support to help you tune in to the music of beauty, abundance and love. Use them, and dance through a life you love.

— Lake Furney

The Joy Will Return
Cameron Johnston

*R*est at last! My tired body and exhausted brain had been looking forward to this day for months. An extremely busy work year was ending and a well-deserved vacation was beginning. We loaded our two daughters into the car and began a long, unstructured camping trip down the eastern seaboard of the US.

We were less than three hours into this long overdue rest and family adventure when the unpredictable nature of years of poorly managed stress, combined with an overworked and unbalanced lifestyle called in a long past due account. As I began to relax, an intense depression descended on me that I would not wish on my worst enemy.

For the next three weeks, I did not have a positive thought. My concentration levels were next to zero. I had never felt so hopeless or scared in my life. At the time, I had no idea what was happening or what to do about it.

I learned that because of years of poorly managed stress my body's energy reserves had used up. My stress load had exceeded my stress coping ability, and the negative balance had reached overload. As I began to relax, an extreme negative reaction suddenly exploded, and I was in serious depression.

If someone had asked me days before if I felt stressed, I would have said no. Tired, frustrated, in need of rest, yes, but not stressed. Stress can be very deceptive. Therefore, we need to be alert to how stress is affecting us and recognize the stress warning signals. I had been having periodic extreme stress warning signals for years, but went on with life as usual, not realizing the danger just around the corner.

Camping beside the ocean, I often walked along the beach trying to figure out what was happening. One thought kept me sane and brought me through this dark time. Simply trust God. He understands, and he will bring healing and work it all out. Many times a day I prayed, "Lord, I do not know what is happening to me, I cannot think clearly, I can't even pray coherently so I am simply going to relax in you and trust you to see me through this."

With rest, change, support from a loving family and the grace of God, the depression lightened. After two months, I thought that I was ready to go back to work, but within hours of arriving home, I realized I was not ready to go back. I finally went to see my doctor and discovered that I was in the later stages of burnout from which it took me three years to fully recover.

I write this today so that others may avoid an unnecessary experience that can literally derail the most noble of purpose. Stress is the spice of life, but excessive stress, combined with poor coping skills and the unbalanced lifestyle of our 24/7 world, can literally kill you!

I also write to share the good news that full recovery from serious burnout is possible. I speak on Cooling Off The Stress Soup and teach skills to develop a stress hardiness needed to enjoy life. I also consult and coach individuals recovering from burnout and bring hope with the good news that a full and complete recovery is possible.

The joy will return.

— Cameron Johnston

Obsession
Susan Paige

I have always been an obsessed soul. My obsessions became my dreams, which became my life. I live my passions. I am married to my best friend and have a career as a teacher, healer, speaker, writer, intuitive and artist. I know I am living my obsessions, because while I am in the act of doing them, like healing or teaching, I feel in a zone. The zone, for me, is a feeling of being in the flow.

But my life was once different. I overcame challenges in my life to get here. Even when I think I have overcome a trauma or challenge, there appears more layers within myself to look at, work through and overcome in order to create the joy when I am living my dreams in the zone. Being in the zone helps me handle the challenges in life more easily.

My life continues to be filled with many opportunities which I have seized giving me the personal growth, skills and knowledge to achieve my dreams. It took me 50 years, and just about as many careers and jobs, to be living my passion today.

Even as a kid, I felt I had healing and intuitive abilities. In order to be accepted, I lead a conservative life with my job choices: management, sales, marketing and real estate.

Fortunately, I did have a few wise elders, my mother and grandmother, in my life who supported my creative side. In my teens, I began my path as a healer. I expanded my knowledge by studying Buddhism, Hinduism, meditation, yoga, healing techniques and natural health. Despite my studies, I stayed in mainstream careers. I had the desire to be a healer, but the comfort level with mainstream jobs was easy and familiar.

At 35, I opened a real estate office in the Chicago area. The stress of the first two years of my business exhausted my body and mind. It was what I needed to make the commitment to be a healer and teacher. I found a two-year certification program that gave me the skills to conduct workshops in personal and spiritual growth. I also took courses in the Reiki, a gentle hands on healing touch. During the time I had my real estate office, I did 24/7 weeks fueled by my passions. At home, I was healer and teacher taking clients and giving workshops. At the office, I was owner and manager, boosting my staff's morale and helping buyers find their dream home. The "at home Susan" helped the "at office Susan."

This lifestyle continued for seven years until my husband came into my life and rushed me off to a new city where, upon allowing the universe to take the lead, I found my dream position. All the parts of Susan could merge as a manger of a large holistic center. This lasted for two years of bliss when we were transferred to yet another new city.

This proved to be the biggest challenge of all for us both. We missed everyone and everything. I fell back to taking conservative jobs, finding it difficult to find like-minded people. A year later, my husband was diagnosed with Leukemia. I clung to my conservative jobs out of financial fear, but still managed to give some of my workshops around town. After four months of chemo, and many months of dread of the future for him, we decided to get off of the roller coaster of fear and eminence and treat his disease as just a part of our lives and not the end of it.

Releasing the fear made room for positive things to appear in our lives. I moved forward with my passion and attended massage school. In the three years since my husband has been in remission, I have created my dreams into my life. I completed massage school and have an active healing practice, managed two wellness centers, given many workshops and teach Reiki and other courses at a massage school. Together we built a beautiful peaceful new home. My deepest dream had been to have a separate healing room as part of my home, which I now have. I ask every day to be a conduit of love and compassion to myself first so that I can be a conduit of love and compassion to my clients and all with whom I come in contact. When I allow this, my life is filled with opportunities.

— Susan H. Paige

To the Top of Mt Fuji
Sylvia M. Sultenfuss

We arrived at base camp on a bus full of runners. We were here because against my better judgment, I had succumbed to my 10-year-old son's pressure to climb Mount Fuji. Lacking warm clothing and the proper physical fitness, we attempted the climb.

At 8 a.m., we started our trek at 6,000 feet. The light wooden pole with a jingle bell attached steadied our steps. My chest began to tighten and my breath was labored within 15 minutes. Soon my son started to complain of shortness of breath. Shoji, the mountain guide, observed us lagging far behind the group, and in his broken English, challenged us, "You want climb to top?"

"If we can," I struggled. "Where is the top?"

Shoji pointed to a small dark dot on the flat top of the hill ahead of us. It was far away, but seemed possible to reach. I nodded.

"Then, do what I say. Take one step at a time and only listen your body. You do what I say, you might get to top."

He turned and began jogging up the mountain with a full pack on his back. I did not question his instructions.

Concentrating on each step, we stuck together – encouraging and keeping each other occupied.

The little black dot I had seen at the top of the horizon of hill called to us. Finally, we saw the small hut ahead. We were offered a cup of tea and an elderly Japanese man offered to brand the meters onto the walking stick.

"Of course, I'm getting my stick stamped," I declared. "I've made it to the top and I'm proud of it!" The wrinkled old body accepted my money and stamped the stick.

I was sitting sipping the hot Jasmine tea when Shoji appeared on the scene. "You made it!" he said, seemingly surprised.

"We sure did!" I proclaimed.

"You want to go to top?" His tone was playfully seductive.

"This is not the top?" I squalled incredulously.

"No. There the top." He pointed again to a small speck of dark on the grayish brown top of the hill.

"Is that really the top?" I challenged, not believing him now.

"That the top," he said decidedly.

Every person who passed us on that mountain had advice. "Don't stop. It's harder to get going again once you have stopped. Keep a steady pace. Don't think about it." The unsolicited recommendations continued. A 100-year-old man celebrating his first climb of the mountain passed us with a steady ease that made me cringe with embarrassment.

"Take one step at a time and listen to only your body," were Shoji's words

There are five sets of branded stamps on the stick. Each burned symbol represented another "top of the mountain," another 1000 meters. The trek up the mountain became more treacherous the higher we climbed. Sometimes our one step forward resulted in a 3-foot slip backward down the path. We slipped and fell, wincing at the impact of the sharp cutting edges of the volcanic rocks. The sunny day brought the discomfort of sweat and thirst. I reminded myself, "Keep moving, one step at a time."

When a big gust of wind thrust my son into a giant boulder that stopped him from being thrown over the mountainside, we were unable to respond with much emotion – his face white with terror, he said nothing. Giving him a gentle hug, I guided him forward. We had no energy to waste on fear.

Finally as we rounded the bend, we heard the noise of celebration from a gathering with folks drinking and eating in front of a tent-like structure. "You made it!" we heard friends scream.

We were not joyous, having no energy to think. The motley four of us had reached the top after nine hours. We were about to collapse when we heard the cries, "They're here, so now we can leave; we must hurry before the storm sets in."

I thought we must now have to rush down the mountain to avoid the terrible sleet that I had read was so common on Mt. Fuji. I was disoriented and could not believe my ears when the chant began. "To the top, to the top!" they shouted in unison. This wasn't the top?

I didn't stop my body. I just kept trudging. "No, Mom. We can stop. Please let's stop here!" my son pleaded.

"We made it this far," I said. "I'll be damned if we're not going to the top. Let's go."

The group was far ahead of us. They ran like billy goats up the hill. The cold, moist fog surrounded us. We could only see a few feet in front of us. The wind and sleet whipped our tired bodies. The trail was more difficult with many large boulders to maneuver around. I felt the danger and didn't care. The mountain was not going to win!

We saw two 10-foot standing poles with a cross bar—a symbol of reaching the top. The wall of gloomy fog surrounded us, and the light of day was passing quickly. Out of the mists came the group of climbers, with our friends out in front. "You made it! I don't believe it. Wow! Quick, let's get a picture and rush down the mountain. The storm is close."

As we began the descent, our muscles quivered with weakness. The wind howled. The sleet snapped and cracked. The shale of crushed rock crunched beneath each step. My feet slipped along the path. And in the midst of the sound of nature's fury, I heard the message that meant more than the conquering of the mountain.

"From now on, I will always know that you are a woman of your word," said my son. "You said we were going to the top, and we did."

"What do you mean?" I retorted. "We did this because you said you had to climb Mt. Fuji."

"Yeah, but I would have stopped a long time ago," he explained.

We had taken only one step at a time. We had listened to our own bodies and listened to the coach. We went to the edge of reality and celebrated each "top" as a goal worth achieving. We made it to the top of the mountain, a spiritual transformation indeed. My relationship with my son had been forever altered.

— Sylvia M Sultenfuss, P. C.

Full of Grace
Kimberly Ann Hasaka

"What is the purpose of life?" asked the Mind. "To live," answered the Soul.

"How shall I live?" questioned the Mind.

The soul explained. "Live as if you are truly alive! Allow yourself to fall in love with life and all its possibilities. Let your senses be filled to the brim of your being! Extend beyond your own physical existence, and let your essence fill the room. Live intentionally, live boldly, courageously, exceptionally, enthusiastically, contagiously and, most of all, passionately!

"Recognize the nobility of your spirit, your soul. Nobility exists and lives undeniably inside each of us. It exists and lives undeniably inside of you. Be careful not to deny yourself what has been yours since birth. We have a way of believing we are less, but we are much more than we realize. You are more too! You were created wonderfully! Refuse to forget. Promise to remember. Tell yourself everyday, if necessary, until you believe it.

"Live with your heart open! Extend love first and foremost to yourself, but don't confuse self- love with being self- centered. One is an action of the heart, the other serves the ego. Only one will bring true happiness, and serve others simultaneously. Love others, but not to your detriment because part of your purpose is to practice self love. How well can you love yourself if you are allowing others to hurt you, or disrespect you? In the moment you decide to love yourself, and truly honor yourself, life will improve. Practice self love.

"Learn to receive love. There is an infinite source of love in this world, an endless supply. Believe you deserve to be loved. Accept it. Embrace it. Receive it. Let others in; accept their love graciously!

"You were born with gifts! Use them. Cultivate them now. Don't let them sleep inside of you, or take them to your grave.

They will be lost forever, and the world will never have known them. When you put your gifts into the world do not think you are finished with your purpose. Look at Whitney Houston, her voice is truly a gift to this world. However, she still struggles with part of her life's purpose: self-love. Learn how to stop self destructive behavior. Don't sabotage your life. Get help when you need it. The world is full of cures.

"Remember your body. You get one. Take care of it.

"Life is short. Move beyond your petty grievances, as well as severe wounds from your most brutal offenders. Heal your wounds. You have an intrinsic ability to heal. Part of your life's purpose is healing. Don't carry anger around with you. It will affect every aspect of your life. It's like being diseased. Learn healthy ways to deal with your anger. Make the decision to let it go. The price of carrying around anger is high and ultimately, you lose. Find peaceful resolutions to conflicts. Transform anger and hatred into love, and understanding. Learn and practice forgiveness; it is part of your life's work. If you need assistance, ask for help. The world is full of amazing resources to help you on life's journey."

The Soul was quiet. The Mind honed in on the silence, in need of more information.

Finally the soul spoke, "You have an incredible ability to over-complicate things, so let me help you. In your lifetime... love yourself and others. Stay open to life. Let wounds heal, push through fear, transform anger, master forgiveness, put your gifts into the world. They were given to you for a reason. Share them. Remember the heavens are not only above you, they surround you. There is a God, and he loves you. He wants you to love you too. Remember self love is not about being self serving. There is a difference. You were created by grace and infused with grace. Now, go forward, and live your life to the fullest with grace."

— Kimberly Ann Hasaka

On-going Journey
Anita Narayan

*L*iving the life I love started when I learned one very fundamental thing –transformation happens when you unlock your potential and develop inner resources.

In March 2000, my career involved very long hours, and I was feeling restricted and unfulfilled. I noticed other things that were extremely important to me were neglected. The lifestyle of freedom I was seeking would not be fulfilled had I remained in my work. I was afraid of failure and lacked self-confidence when it came to starting a business – something about the security of a pay check. There was not an external event that could give me the confidence I needed. These were issues left to inner resources. My mindset and outlook began to change when I attended a Tony Robbins event at Wembley called "Unleash the Power Within."

It was this event that began my journey to accessing tools to strengthen my inner resources and unlock my potential. I learned how to motivate myself toward change.

My first change was to invest in my own personal development. I attended a university life mastery course. Like driving a car, the real learning came after I got the piece of paper. I continued to expose myself to the things I had already learned so the lessons would take root and recondition my thinking. After all, old habits die hard. I learned and practiced accelerated techniques to aid my absorption and assimilate new knowledge.

I have a passion for football, personal development and health. Since March 2000, I have gone on to start my own life coaching business, and I now specialize in accelerated learning techniques and peak performance coaching. Through my life coaching practice, I take joy in seeing the lives of others transformed personally and professionally. By applying principles of peak performance I extended my career in women's league football and at 40 years-old, I was picked again to play for the region. I have earned a certificate in football coaching.

Living the life I love is not a destination but an on-going journey. There are some key lessons I have learned along the way which have proved instrumental in the lifestyle I am now cultivating and which I continue to learn and translate. I have learned to ask different questions of my life. I now ask "How Can I?" instead of "Can I?" The brain responds to questions just like a computer responds to a search for a keyword and will seek to answer that question.

I have also learned that environment is important to growth. I have surrounded myself with quality friends who share and cultivate similar core values such as honesty, fun, empathy, positive outlook, contribution to others, compassion and growth. A tool that has had great impact on my growth has been the Centerpointe Program, which uses sound technology through passive listening to induce states of deep rest and relaxation while helping my brain evolve to higher levels of functioning. This has enabled me to acknowledge and release emotions rather than suppress them. I have acquired deeper states of calm and composure during challenging times.

Having a personal coach has given me the synergy and focus to aid my endeavours. I have also learned to see failure and mistakes as an important part of the fabric of success rather than its antithesis. I compare life to football. It is a contact sport where there is a clear goal of winning the match but also an acceptance that I will get tackled at some stage. I have discovered that when I let go of what I cannot control, I access a more resourceful state where creative energy helps me find resolution, solutions and new possibilities.

I have shared with you joys and challenges in the hope that you can see that living the life you love is not about smooth sailing. It is exciting nevertheless. What ultimately determines our experience in life depends on our inner resources and commitment to growth. Growth brings its new opportunities along with a fruitful and exciting life. There is no other place I would rather be!

— Anita Narayan

No One Looks Forward to December 26
James A. Sapp

*T*hey laughed. "Now, what stupid idea does Jim have?" I can still remember like it was yesterday; people laughing about a new business I was starting.

The year was 1995, and I had decided to sell vitamins. Shortly after I made this decision, a friend I worked with at Rockwell/ Boeing Corporation, Bob Thompson, suggested, "Why don't you market your vitamins on the Internet?"

Have you ever had a light bulb go off in your brain? Well, this was one of those moments.

There was one slight problem: I knew absolutely nothing about the Internet. That seemed, however, like a small speed bump on the road I wanted to travel. My belief was so strong that, even after having invested over 400 hours of work to earn $22, I wasn't discouraged in the least. I had a vision of where I was headed and nothing was going to stop me.

A year and a half later I had more than doubled my income as an engineer with Rockwell Corp.

I had become the first person in my network marketing company to rise to the Diamond level while holding a full time job. Eventually I would walk into my manager's office and resign. I had become one of my company's top distributors because I had a belief that started with a simple seed and grew into a mighty oak.

This was accomplished because I very good at Internet marketing and search engine positioning. However, these achievements are relatively small compared to the promise of my current vision. It is all because of a simple secret I discovered.

As a kid, why did you never have trouble getting up on Christmas morning? There are two reasons: first, you knew that something really good was going to happen to you, and, second, you had an unshakeable belief that there would be presents under the tree. Hence the great excitement and anticipation, creating a great, positive attitude.

The secret of extraordinary people are excited to get up every day and so should we. By believing something great will happen each day, we bring together unseen forces to help us. This attitude attracts the right people to aid us in accomplishing great things.

Anybody can get excited over something good that's a sure deal – like Christmas. However, what separates the extraordinary from the ordinary is the vision to see what others can't see in the future and take action.

There are two roads in life. One is a very broad, well-paved road and the amazing thing about this road is that you don't have to look for it to find it. By simply doing nothing, it will find you and, in 40 years or less, it will take you to the twin over-populated cities of Regret and Failure.

On the other hand, there is another road that is much harder to find. It's simply a bare unmarked trail at the beginning, and many people walk past it everyday without noticing. But once in a while it offers a glimpse of the great vision that waits at trail's end.

The great thing about being on this second road is that you meet other travelers who make traveling easier and considerably more fun.

Everyone on this road sees something fascinatingly different "on down the road." Walt Disney saw Disneyland and Epcot Center on this road. Orville and Wilbur Wright could see the future of air travel. Henry Ford could see a nation of automobiles. Our founding fathers could see a land of free men in a country that was the greatest land of freedom and opportunity the world had ever known.

So, if you dare, we invite you to take this "Journey of No Regrets," where the hardest step is always the first.

— James A. Sapp

The Empowerment of Passion
Rob Luka

When I was a child, I had recurring nightmares. I would wake up visibly shaken and both of my parents would come running into the room. Even when the dreams persisted, my fear was such that my parents never took turns getting up in the middle of the night. They both continued to comfort me.

Eventually, I grew out of the dreams and they came with less intensity and frequency. Even as an adult however, I never became fully aware of the encrypted message that the same repetitious dream was trying so hard to deliver – until I met John, a hypnotherapist. He offered me his skill in an attempt to bring understanding and insight into interpreting its meaning. Regressing me gently, back to the age of six, together we discovered the vital purpose this nightmare served. Intuitively, I knew my parents were heading for a divorce. Those dreams, and the fear created by them, not only brought my parents together but right by my side. I didn't have to go to them, and they gave me their attention together instead of separately. Pretty sharp for a kid, wouldn't you say? I wish I had stayed that smart as an adult!

John helped lay to rest that chapter in my life. Meeting John, forever peaked my curiosity and interest in hypnotherapy. I went on to learn and study with the best: Elizabeth Kubler Ross, Brian Weiss, Roger Woolger and Paul Hansen all made significant contributions to my training. It's amazing how personal obstacles frequently appear as opportunities begging to be looked upon as such.

In 1981, in search of a deeper spiritual understanding, I moved to India. For three months I lived steeped in a spiritual, self-reflective, meditative lifestyle while living in an ashram. The experience of looking directly into the eyes of an enlightened spiritual master was more than profound. I never felt such peace, contentment and stillness of thought. I was a Westerner learning

Eastern approaches to mind and spirit, and had the unique opportunity to unite the two.

When I began working with children in my career as a registered nurse, I would often be faced with kids who were scared to death of medical procedures. I could easily relate to their fear, and now I had the experience, tools and training to do something about it. My own experience as a child, learning hypnotherapy and the profound impact of India, seemed to combine into a sort of ready mixed formula. My passion became the shifting of children from a state of fear to a position of empowerment. Dismantling their fear and then watching them go through a medical procedure calmly became a "high" for me.

Now, as I find myself in life's transition, no longer a bedside nurse, the passion continues. Empowering children in fear is now a book in progress, which shares touching stories, techniques and children's own responses while making the shift from fear to empowerment.

What do you fear? What stands in your way to living an empowered life that you love? Take yourself on – and let it fly. Peace.

— Robert Luka

There are Only Obstacles to Overcome, Never Roadblocks
Samuel L. Sykes

What are you passionate about? Your passion is as personal as your fingerprint. It's the thing that really matters to you; you care enough that it involves commitment and risk. In How Much Joy Can You Stand?: A Creative Guide to Facing Your Fears and Making Your Dreams Come True, Suzanne Falter-Barns says, "The truth is that dreams can be both tantalizing and frightening. They call upon us to be our bigger selves, possibly bigger than we've ever been...so we extend our reach out into the world and finally begin to touch our lives as we are meant to."

I grew up in a tight-knit, loving family that stressed to me the importance of a strong work ethic. I remember my parents and grandparents telling me, "If you work hard and do what you need to do, good things will happen." During my teens, while my friends were out playing, I would ride my bicycle for two miles on snow covered roads to do chores for a local farmer. I was always committed to broadening my skills and knowledge, progressing from farm work to being a lumberjack, to leaving a family construction business that was already established for me, to traveling the world and absorbing all the international experiences and challenges that would await me in corporate America.

I knew that by staying in the corporate world, I was only shortchanging myself. I was looked down upon by many of those around me for the failures that happened, despite the fact that I never gave up. I tried to learn something positive from each failure or defeat and move on. It was my grandmother who never lost faith in me. She always said that she wanted to see me make my first million dollars before she died. It was 2 years ago that I lost her at the age of 90. I kept every one of her letters and gifts that I had received from her for the past 10 years, as they inspired me to keep moving forward. Even though she was no longer with me, I knew that she would forever be in my heart, and I set out with renewed energy to realize that dream.

Understanding that I still had much to learn, I sought to associate myself with those who had already become successful so that I could further broaden my knowledge and contacts. I always gave everyone the benefit of the doubt and sought to treat them with openness and honesty. It was unfortunate that, throughout the years, unethical people who had nothing to offer took advantage and abused my energy, charm and contacts. These were challenging years, but I felt that we were designed and created for extraordinary achievement.

God puts a dream in your heart and gives you all the gifts, talents and hidden resources you'll need to make your dream come true. It is up to you to do the work. It is up to each one of us to decide to make the journey, to put ourselves through the struggle and pursue our dreams. When we are struggling, we will dig deep inside and only then will we find our gifts. Despite the setbacks, I persevered until I met the person who made a difference in my life, my business partner, James Bolin. He believed in me and offered me the opportunity that has today become known as Secondary Capital Network. SCN has the stated goal of becoming the "world's largest trade network," and with the quality of people in our organization, achieving that goal is certainly within reach.

The founding of SCN was driven by the realization that trade has never reached its full potential and we have set out to offer an alternative solution. Our motto is, "In a world of unfulfilled promises, a solution has arrived that carries a vision of the future and will change forever the way people think about trade." SCN is setting the standards of excellence in the trade world by finally fulfilling the promises.

Today, my grandmother would be proud. I have achieved the financial success she always felt I would achieve, but, just as importantly, I have found my passion and purpose. You owe it to yourself to heed and pursue your dreams. Sure, it'll be a challenge, but the exhilaration of facing your fears is more energizing than the feeling of unrealized potential. I've never heard of anyone who regretted following their heart.

— Samuel L. Sykes

Crying Makes Me Happy!
Dianea Kohl

M y greatest fear was feeling and crying, especially in front of others. Even though my mother cried in front of us, there was always an air of shame around this natural response to hurt. It was like honey hidden in a comb, no taste, only feeling the dislike of its stickiness.

Tears stuck on my blue irises as I stood face-to-face with my tenth grade math teacher to explain that I thought he had incorrectly marked one of my answers wrong. Other students stood waiting as I felt the hot sting in my eyes, fighting not to expose my tears. The memory is as vivid as the pain I stored inside. Over and over again, I hid my tears. I was afraid to be criticized for my vulnerability. My human heart.

I saw my grandmother cry only once, tears slowly making their groove down her cheek as she looked at photos of her eldest son, years after he had died in a hit-and-run accident at the age of 21. I was silent. I had no idea what to say. No idea what to do.

I never saw my father cry – maybe tears welled up once as he said goodbye to me when I left for college. In the past decade, I've allowed myself to feel so many tears over missing opportunities to cry with him, to share all of ourselves. I loved him more so now.

Just last night, I watched the video, *Bounce*, and was aghast when the adult daughter told her mother not to cry, when they learned of the death of her husband. Can this fear still exist in this new millennium?

My granddaughter, Denali, and I share tears whenever they arise, and they have connected us like stars with the moon. When she was six, visiting her other grandmother in California, she called me in New York, asking me to talk to her grandma Ruth. "Tell her it's okay that I cry, and that I don't have to go to my room. That it's no big deal!" I was so surprised; I jumped for joy! Denali actually had to call her mom in Baltimore in order to find my phone number.

Yes, out of the mouth of babes comes the truth – a truth I model for my family since my heart cracked open during my fourth marriage. I have two daughters from my first marriage to Chuck, which ended when he could admit his gayness, denied by our strict religious upbringing as "born again" Christians. My second marriage to Reid ended when I was able to hear my own heart, the doubt since age 10 that my religious upbringing was not the one-way to God, and I flew free. A few years after our friendly divorce, he learned he had cancer and died at the young age of 44.

My third marriage, to Alain, came after living with him for a year, believing he had changed, stopped smoking and reduced his drinking. After six months of marital therapy, he didn't want to change, and I needed the intimacy of shared feelings. Marriage number four to Gregory careened me into feelings I had not known existed within me, pain I had covered up with religious brainwashing. Since I was a toddler in weekly Sunday school, I had heard that I was born in sin, unworthy of God's love. I have cried many tears over that retrieved memory of emotional pain that nearly crushed my innocent child's loving spirit.

Thankfully, I have awakened from that denial by allowing God-given tears, our body's natural process for sharing our hearts and healing. Since then, I have allowed my rage to be a surfboard. Innocent tears that have washed away my anger and brought true compassion for others. My judgementalness has turned into love of a deeper order. But now my fear of being true in my heart and the fear of being "real" in my life are subsiding. And as a therapist working with and healing others, my mission is to pass this on to everyone. I live to unshame tears, as Rumi, a 13th century poet said, "When the shell of my heart breaks open, tears shall pour forth and they shall be called the pearls of god." May we all find that freedom, those "pearls of god," that vulnerability that heals our heart.

Never fear tears; never fear your feelings. Revel in life – a gift so great that it must make you cry.

— Dianea Kohl

Allow Your Purpose to Surface
Ann M. Preston

"**W**hat do you want to be when you grow up?" Ask this question to any child and they will say things like become an astronaut, a movie star or a famous ball player!

Where is that dream now? Just because you may be in your 40's and you sell "widgets" doesn't mean your dream is not somewhere deep inside of you. I believe everyone has a purpose. They just need to allow it to surface.

Several years ago I lost someone I loved very much. She was like a daughter to me and I was devastated. While I was deciding what to do next, I picked up Deepak Chopra's book, The Seven Spiritual Laws of Success. While reading his book, I got the idea that would change my life. I found my purpose. It was within me all along!

You see, life has a way of beating us down and forcing us to conform to ordinary roles. It's just like the story about the goldfish. He can only grow to a certain size, depending upon the size of his fishbowl. Move him to a beautiful outdoor pond, however, and he can grow one hundred times the size.

I had been a shy, scared, tiny goldfish living inside my tiny, little fishbowl. When I allowed my purpose to surface, I rediscovered my childhood passion for being a leader among the other kids, for directing and putting on shows in our basement and for never losing a race – even against a boy.

Now, I am a successful entrepreneur who teaches others how to realize their dreams and succeed through the system I created the day I found my purpose.

I am a leader of thousands of business people. I produce life-altering shows with world-class speakers, and whenever I have a challenge in my business or in my personal life, I never lose a race! My greatest passion is to help others succeed. My purpose and my organization, Freedom Builders, provides a forum for others to build their business and stretch their vision every day. My dream has grown from creating the best business success system ever created to completely revolutionizing the sales process worldwide by spreading Freedom Builders concept of The New Way to Sell all across the globe!

I couldn't have created such a massive system without "the other kids on the block." Once you've allowed your purpose to surface, you need to share it with others. People are our greatest gifts. Don't be afraid to share your dream because, when you do, the person sitting next to you could be the one to make that dream come true.

Create a Team and Realize Your Dream.

T. Together vs. apart (in mind, spirit & outcome)
E. Everyone participates fully
A. Admit your shortcomings
M. Make each other's dreams come true
W. Willing to do for others as much as for yourself
O. Overcome hurdles together
R. Recognize, reward and restore each other
K. Keep sharing this concept until there's no one left to share it with

So don't wait until life stops you to find your purpose. Take the day off, relax and allow your purpose to surface today. Then share it with others and make it happen.

Here's To You!

— Ann M. Preston

The Most Important Thing!
Kimberly Mac

O ne of the most important things in life is to love what you do. When you are living what you are truly passionate about, life seems like a dream. You can work 18 hours a day, and it doesn't feel as if any time has passed. When you love something, all time stops, there are no limits and you are present in the moment. That is living life! Or is it?

I was in love with my job in every way. My life seemed perfect, except for one thing. I didn't have a life outside of my job, creating an imbalance that, over time, creates illness. Balance is essential for health and longevity.

In August of 1994, I learned the importance of balance when I was suddenly stricken with a debilitating illness; I was not even able to walk. For nine and a half months I was in the dark, in the hands of dozens of doctors who had no idea of what was wrong or what my body needed. I was helpless in excruciating pain, and did not know whether I would ever walk or even stand on my own again. I thought, "Why me?" I would think about all the things I had always wanted to do, but never did. I would think about death and what it meant. What would I do if I knew that I was dying? How would I live if I knew that I was dying? I realized that I would not be living the way that I had been living.

This illness gave me a chance for a new life, even if I didn't know it at that time.

The doctors inadvertently had given me a challenge by their diagnosis of the incurable disease, Fibromyalgia, and their remedy of medication everyday for the rest of my life. The challenge: Drugs and their incurable diagnosis would rule my life. I decided I would be in control.

These are the key steps I took in order to regain my health and my life. I believe these are essential to living a healthy life with purpose.

Step #1: Belief that I could heal by my own will.

Nothing is going to be in control of me. Taking a stand for myself was my first step to healing. My belief in my own ability to heal myself started me on a journey to healing with my intuition as my guide.

We have choices: the choice to choose the life we desire to live, the life we are meant to live or we choose not. Either way, we choose.

Step #2: Awareness and recognition of the power of things when they are given to me.

It took some years to understand the reason why I had Fibromyalgia. I believe that I was given a gift in having this illness. As a result, I was guided to take control of my own destiny. It stopped me from using everyone and everything as an excuse not to live the life that I was meant to live. Since I appeared to be the healthiest person everyone knew, it was a shock that I, of all people, would be ill. With this, I understood my power in having Fibromyalgia was to teach others how to make health their priority.

Step #3: Decide and take action for what I want.

I decided that I would be in control of my health for the rest of my life. This decision was what led me to cure myself of Fibromyalgia. Holistic health education became my primary focus, followed with active steps for real results. As I learned, health does not remain if you fail to take action to keep it.

Living healthy is my key to youth and longevity. Without health, all the money, family, friends and time means nothing since you can't enjoy them.

Know the power you have inside you. You can achieve anything you desire. Just believe in yourself. Follow your belief with passion, education and action to get everything you want in life.

— Kimberly Mac

Be Willing To Walk Away and Follow Your Passion
Dr. Nell Rodgers

*P*eople loved me. I could feel it. Clients reported miracles. I worked hard and diligently. My bank account was healthy. I ran three miles daily, meditated each morning and chose healthy foods. I traveled the world, and my home was a haven. Colleagues, friends and clients respected me. People traveled from across America to avail themselves of my work. I had it all.

Why, then, did I feel restless, extremely tired, frustrated and unfulfilled? Why did I have little interest in life? I loved my clients and my work. But I felt my spirit was shriveling? Why did I seek freedom when, by external standards, I was living the blessed life? I felt shackled. I attended more seminars, studied harder and extended myself in service. I recorded my struggle in my journal. I prayed. I wept when alone at night. I suppressed myself and refused to acknowledge my innermost passion. I became ill but still compelled my body to return to the office, willing myself to continue.

When engaged with a client, implementing my skills, I felt terrific. But underneath, the yearning, longing and angst were ever present. I wanted to be free. As my spiritual quest led to deeper understandings, I began to see that I would never be free until I honored my heart-song. I love teaching, singing and acting. My career choice would have been one of these had my father permitted it. I was a victim, longing for what might have been. My misery kept me from moving, and lack of movement made me miserable. While I expressed joy, positivity, a hopeful outlook and felicity to my clients and friends, I was heartsick.

To feed my hungry spirit, I took acting lessons. As impossible as it seemed, I won a role with every audition. On stage, I felt spirited and filled with passion. But, how could I leave a thriving practice, a handsome income, a life of prestige? How could I desert the clients I loved, who depended upon me, who loved me? How could I cast off this "optimal" life and step into nothing? I was unwilling to walk away. Ultimately, sheer fatigue and weariness from internal conflict forced me to sell my practice.

I was free! I was still respected, loved and revered. I had time to sing, write and be on stage. The support from my friends and colleagues was amazing. They honored that I had found the courage to walk away. Some took my lead and left jobs in which they were miserable. Without fail, each of us has been rewarded for our willingness to honor the fire within; to create a life which is aligned with the inner spirit and passion.

Walking away is not necessarily easy. Nor will every person in your life support you. Some will think you are crazy or question your motives. Craziness is staying in a situation which drains energy, squelches desire, blots out creativity and sucks away life. Sanity comes with integrity, personal fulfillment and a commitment to the soul's longings.

Delaying a decision to walk away prolongs agony. Be willing to love yourself enough to shed your misery. The personal work of altering or releasing deep-seated beliefs may be tedious and intense, and the rewards not immediately obvious. Walking away, however, can bring personal power, renewed passion and a spirit which is free to explore and become all that you desire to be. Time may be required to set your feet firmly and happily onto a new path. Nevertheless, your soul will be nurtured.

I have established a situation which allows me to see clients if I wish, or see no one; something everyone thought impossible. I travel the world and still serve humanity. The difference is that my spirit is thriving and I am doing what I love. I am alive!

"Nothing is more powerful than gentleness."

Puppet or Puppeteer:
You Hold the Key to the Life You Really Love

— Dr. Nell

Childhood Dreams, Adults Wake Up
Bruce de Torres Towers

I was afraid so I decided to be an actor. I was in the sixth grade.

We did a "Roaring Twenties" variety show. I played Jack Dempsey, the boxer. I was so excited, I punched my scene partner off the stage.

My father was in the audience. The man next to him said, "Geez, that kid is really hitting him." My father didn't know what to say.

My father's Spanish. My mother's Cuban. I've always been passionate. That doesn't mean I knew what I was doing.

All my life, people said I was lucky. I knew what I wanted to do. Inside, however, I was suffering. I could get big parts, but I ruined myself in rehearsal. By the time I got on stage, I stunk.

But I was determined.

I had a breakthrough. Yeah. After years of performing in play after play. It was amazing. I started getting cast in everything I auditioned for, or so it seemed. The New York Times said I was the funniest and most vocally gifted member of a uniformly fine cast. What happened? I started paying attention. I mean, I only paid attention. And that made all the difference.

Sure, I did what we rehearsed, but now I was in sync with my scene partners. We could let magic happen. It was incredible.

Then something strange started to happen. I saw how unhappy I was. So I decided to learn how to be happy. My lifeline was to pay attention. That always worked.

Then my friend Bob gave me *Think And Grow Rich* by Napoleon Hill. When we're ready the teacher appears. (Well, the teacher is always around. When we're ready, we see him or her.) There's nothing but energy. Okay. Thoughts are things. Okay. But why do thoughts made of energy become things in real life? Do they want to? Did energy burst into existence and become us because it wanted to? Are we and energy and everything we think and see made of the intention to exist?

That was a light-bulb. I decided to write a book in order to master these ideas and, more importantly, become who writing such a book would make me.

Energy moves and gathers into things. Energy goes where we throw attention. We give life to what we give attention to. Consciousness creates.

Our thoughts and feelings become people, places and things because they're made of energy. We're always creating. Welcome to heaven.

That's right. Heaven. It goes deeper.

There's only one of us here. Energy is just another word for love. Love is all there is.

We – for lack of a better word – are playing a game. We are pretending to be separate people. There is no you. There is no me. There's only love. We're looking in a mirror. We're talking to ourself. This appearing to be you and me is an illusion. So pay attention.

The universe is our body. The universe is a projection, a creation, an emanation from and of our subconscious. Change the deep beliefs and feelings in our subconscious and the universe changes. Or, as Wayne Dyer likes to say, "Change the way we look at things and the things we look at change." We regain control of the universe by knowing, as we look at it, it's us.

The only sane way to deal with a universe of love is with love.

Two thousand years ago a man got nailed to a cross. He said, "Forgive them; they know not what they do." They didn't know they were love. They never matured past a child's understanding of you versus me. It's urgent we learn to love. It's urgent we speak and create intentionally. The universe takes what we think and gives it back to us as people, places and things. The trick is to breathe and relax and connect with our bodies and, through them, with the rest of us, which is infinite. There is no place where you stop and I begin. To know us is to love us because the real us, under these masks, is love.

We must have wanted someone to talk to. Why else would we manifest ourselves as people who must have conversations to get along and share love? What helps us have conversations better than paying attention to each other?

To give love is the only way to feel it. Stay in touch.

— Bruce de Torres Towers

The $25,000.00 Dollar Knock
Jeffery Craig Shirley

We have all read, heard or seen on TV how others have taken advantage of opportunity when it knocked. When was the last time opportunity knocked on your door? Think about that for a minute now!

One day, while visiting a friend at home, the doorbell rang; I went to the door. A woman was standing there, and she introduced herself as the financee of Jim, the owner of the property next door. She said, "I noticed you had your house up for sale. Did you sell it already?"

"No," I told her, "the owner took the house off the market and plans to sell it at a later date." I continued the conversation by asking her why she was interested.

She replied, "We are interested in selling the property next door when the renters move out at the end of the month and are looking for a quick sale because the young men living there trashed the place."

"May I ask what are you selling the property for?"

She replied, "One hundred seventy-five thousand dollars."

I had a good idea of what property sold for in the neighborhood, and I knew this was quite a reduction of the retail price. I said, "Not to offend you, but I will offer $170,000.00 in cash, one week from today, if you sign a contract today!"

She replied, "Let me speak with Jim, and we will let you know tomorrow."

Before she left that evening, we exchanged phone numbers. After speaking with Jim, he assured me I would be hearing from him. The next day I waited patiently. Then, I received a call asking me what would be a good time to come by to sign a contract.

It was a great relief to Jim to be free of the property. He no longer had to be available all hours of the day to show the property to potential buyers. Jim told me that his father, who lived in California, was the real owner, and he planned to give the money to him. Jim wasn't in a hurry to get the money, even though his tenants were moving out in two weeks and he knew he would have to make the next mortgage payment. He was relieved he wouldn't have to make any payments after that.

After speaking with him for a short time, he agreed to let me go in after the tenants moved out to start my renovation. We had the understanding that if I didn't close by the end of the month, I would make the mortgage payment.

This was really turning into a win-win situation. Thank God for that! I had to make only one mortgage payment before I sold the property for a profit of $25,000. And, I never had the $170,000 to pay cash in 7 days. I only had my faith in the means to locate OPM (other people's money).

Looking at a cup of water, I like to see it half-full, as opposed to half-empty. Anyone can see it half-empty. The key is to surround yourself with people who have a positive mental attitude. That attitude alone will give you the energy you need to step out with faith. Now, ask yourself, "How many people do you know would have answered the door ready to jump on an opportunity?" How would you have answered the door? Would you have been quick to turn her away? Opportunity knocks everyday in so many different ways whether you're dealing with real estate or not. Are you willing to listen and explore with great boldness when opportunity knocks. Opportunity's knuckles are raw from knocking on your door. Will you take time today and listen?

— Jeffery Craig Shirley

"And God Said..."
Chula Schlesinger

"The cyst is benign. I'm just going to drain it and everything will be all right." The doctor reassured me as he prepared for the procedure.

I said, "Okay."

That was the last word I spoke in a normal voice. A cyst on the right lobe of my thyroid gland necessitated the procedure which should have been a walk in the park; instead it led me down a path in the dark. The nerve to my right vocal chord was damaged, leaving it paralyzed. I did not speak above a whisper for three years.

The usual questions of "Why me?" and "How could this happen?" plagued me often. However, the still small voice that had, for years, lead me through life-altering changes and life threatening dangers urged me to avoid self pity. As a former television talk show host, it was frightening to be unable to communicate. Through my personal metamorphosis, my thoughts and feelings began to find their way to my pen.

The biggest question that gnawed at me was "How do I find my voice?" After being told by numerous doctors and speech therapists there was nothing I could do, my stubborn streak brought out the fighter in me. I worked hard at speech exercises and used therapeutic grade essential oils to rejuvenate the nerve. Today, my voice is still soft, but audible; tires easily but is strong enough to move an audience to action.

The most important thing I have learned is each of us must find our own voice. The creation of the universe began with a word. "And God said...." The word was the impetus for all life in its myriad of complexities. We are beings of light and frequency, and the very essence of our being is projected in our thoughts, reflected in our actions and begins with the words we mentally entertain and speak aloud to others. Words solidify our thoughts, giving them form and substance. They direct our actions by repetition and gathering energy.

We must be mindful of our self-talk, as well as what we say to others. Words of encouragement and confidence in another can lift up their belief in themselves to the very heights they may need to overcome their adversities. Learning to be gentle with ourselves will increase our awareness of how we command the creative energy at our disposal. Every word produces an effect just as surely as a tossed pebble produces ever expanding ripples on a lake.

If you do not feel that you have a voice, that you must follow another's lead and have no say in the creation of your personal world, RISE UP! Fight your fears and save yourself. You are the only person with whom you must spend eternity. You are the only person whom you must satisfy at the day's end that you have accomplished your tasks to the best of your ability, and earned your daily bread with honor and dignity. Your thoughts, words and actions are the most important legacy you can leave to those you love. Don't they deserve to know what you really think and who you really are?

Sometimes it is difficult for us to harness the power of our inner voice. Many times fear of changing, or of being rejected, can stop us short of finding our true self. Voicing our belief in ourselves, others or in a creative universal presence on a regular basis, gets easier when we make the commitment to communicate by writing in a journal, meeting regularly at church or sharing with a trusted friend.

One of the exercises I enjoy sharing is "The Left Handed Day." If you are predominately right handed, pick a day out of the week to do everything, literally everything, with your left hand. This simple exercise engages areas of the brain that otherwise would not be stimulated. When I first began doing this, I noticed many long buried memories surfaced, and I was able to reconnect and clear some of my childhood traumas.

This exercise requires extreme concentration, and helps to cut down on the negative self-talk that our mental tape is continuously playing. When we have to stop and focus on what we are doing instead of running on auto-pilot, it puts things in a new and interesting perspective.

Becoming aware of our negative self-talk and bringing it to the foreground is the first step in finding our true voice. Having the courage to speak our truth will facilitate a quantum leap in the way we perceive and trust ourselves. God initiated the creation of entire universes with the utterance of one word. Surely, we can follow this example and find our own voice, creating our world anew and remaking it into one of joy, abundance and prosperity.

— Chula Schlesigner

Focus on Your Passion And Turn It into Your Income!
Caryl T. Lenahan

I can still remember the cold, January night in Denver when I was going to a seminar, "Creating 1991." I felt intuitively drawn there for a larger reason than setting goals. At the end of the evening, we were asked to go into meditation and then write several words that had come to us. I found myself writing "teacher." This didn't make sense! For 14 years I had been very successful in insurance and investment sales, a significant accomplishment as few women were in commissioned sales in the 70's and 80's. My mother had been a teacher all her life, but, like many children, I had pooh-poohed the idea of following in her vocational footsteps.

A year and a half later, I moved to warm Florida, and soon found that a number of people in my church were deeply in debt and desperate for help. I offered a workshop called "How to Get Out of Debt." When the workshop was finished, I knew I would be the life support for some 54 people and their families. To my surprise, I found passion in teaching, cheerleading and making financial strategies interesting. I had discovered my true purpose and a way to combine my writing, people skills, a master's degree in counseling and years in financial services.

The big question was, "If I changed from selling to advising, could I make the kind of income I was used to?" Today, I have multiple streams of income. I am financial advisor, cheerleader, coach and a budget counselor, and I create financial courses and workbooks for my publishing company, Money Miracles. I am truly an entrepreneur doing the many things I love and do best.

My purpose today is, "empowering people to have what they want in life by taking their power back from money." I live by Dr. Robert Schuller's guidance, "Find a need and fill it," and I am continually teaching new financial strategies for helping people "win" their money game. As technology provides the public with wonderful financial tools and information, I am able to offer my financial strategies and materials by tele-seminars and on the Internet.

Since September 11, people have a new sense of urgency about living their lives to the fullest. Dr. Wayne Dyer tells us, "We're all born with a divine plan within us and part of life's challenge is letting it come out. Do not die with your music still in your soul." When I have clients and students who are frustrated about their work or income, I encourage them to create their own "job" by taking the things they do best and creating products and services that people need and will gladly buy. We set up trial methods using their expertise as a business to see how it feels and to determine its profitability. I'm thrilled to see how many are "doing what they love and creating the income they deserve." They just needed a coach and cheerleader!

For those of us willing to step outside our small, worn-out career box, there are vastly bigger, more rewarding fields waiting for us in which to bundle our expertise and the things that give us "juice." When President John F. Kennedy proclaimed, "Ask not what your country can do for you, but rather what you can do for your country," we received a powerful directive for creating our own job titles and sharing our full potential through our work.

Is it your time to refocus and create the new you? I encourage you to knock down the walls of the box that's been holding you prisoner. Seek the purpose and the work you were meant to have. As the number one author of your life, you'll soon be experiencing greater focus, confidence, passion and prosperity. You won't die with your music still in your soul. Your soul's music will be gloriously heard each day as you fully express yourself through your self-chosen work and lifestyle.

— Caryl T. Lenahan

'The Love Guy' Helps Bring Your Relationship with Money into Balance
Dan Klatt

I wrote my first book when I was about 12. Space Soap told the story of "pennies and dimes" at war with the bulky "nickels and quarters" and was waged vividly in my imagination. Out of college, the only jobs I found were in newspapers. I put my love for writing to good use. I was making a difference by informing people of local and national issues affecting them and helping them make the right choices at the ballot.

Ten years later, I decided to go down a different career path; a business for myself in Internet marketing. I contacted an author whose work had helped my personal growth, to help him sell more books online. No paying job, yet he was glad to let me volunteer!

As an early Christmas present, he gave me a statue of Quan Yin, a figure in Buddhism similar to Mother Mary. I had never heard of her before then.

On Christmas Day I did a meditation that was passed around online, and while my eyes were closed, I imagined meeting her and hearing her say, "Why don't you channel a book?"

"Talking" among the other invited guests at this re-creation of the Last Supper, I had this imagined sense that St. Germaine suggested I ask Quan Yin to guide me in writing this book, and I turned and there she was:

"I thought you'd never ask" was her reply. Then she said, "Who do you think made arrangements for you to get that statue?"

My first published book, *Experience Unconditional Love* This Year was born. As the book seemed to flow out of me (in 44 hours, over 30 days) my relationship with my fianceé was becoming excessively challenging. I was able to master unconditional love at the same time the book was showing me how to teach it to others.

Did you notice the similarities among the "coincidental" events?
I had a passion for writing since my youth.
The only jobs I found taught me to master writing and editing.
A "random" gift led me to become a published author,
A workbook and six CDs later, I evolved into "The Love

Guy" relationship coach, also creating the *10-Minute Love Plan* book and volumes of new material.

Yet, as my own interests shifted into creating what I now call The Abundant Mind, or prosperity consciousness, I realized how hard people work just to get by; they don't have the energy or time to become Casanova.

When I started guiding people to become more prosperous through mastering the thoughts they put out there, the miracles really started happening, and they continue now almost on a daily basis.

Love has always been the most important thing to me, yet through the transformation I experienced with my first book, I mastered loving and valuing myself, too. And then, I attracted my true love, and we're still incredibly happy today.

After that, there was nothing more for me to learn, and it seemed like such an effortless transition from helping people love themselves and create the perfect relationship, to loving themselves and bringing their relationship with money back into balance.

There may be different stepping stones along your path, and it may seem to take you away from your goal. Yet, if you stay on the path that unfolds easily in front of you, you will pick up the right experiences to shape who you are.

As you learn, grow and become more, you'll be able to reach the next level, where the next leg of the journey then unfolds easily in front of you.

It starts with honoring your passion and working on becoming the best "you" you can be. Then just keep your eyes, ears and intuition open and receptive to the greater learning – perhaps even the greater purpose.

That's when you'll experience yourself living!

— Dan Klatt

The Secret of Success
Alfonso Desoto

*I*n order to achieve success we need to have a purpose in our lives. Most people do not know their purpose, but there is good news: all of us are born with a definite purpose. God plants a purpose inside of us, and our job is to find it. He does not leave us alone in this task. He gives us hints, precious gifts that come enveloped in our dreams.

Dreams are little voices guiding our journey to achieve our purpose. They begin as a whisper and grow little by little. We can struggle, shrink, shake or cry, but if the dream is there, we will wake up every morning with a smile in our face, feeling unstoppable.

Twenty years ago, I came to this country in search of the American dream. I had recently graduated from architectural school. I had only $300 in my pocket but my head was full of dreams of becoming successful in the "land of opportunities." I could picture my every dream becoming a reality. I struggled, cried and prayed to keep my dream alive because it is my dream that fuels the purpose of my life.

Our dreams are our greatest asset. Before we can reach them, we are taken apart and put together. When God feels that we are humble enough, we will receive the most wonderful gift of all -- the wonderful miracle of our dreams coming true.

After struggles, successes and almost bankruptcy, I had to face not only the creditors that were after me but the sickness of my newborn baby. The stress from these situations originated a panic attack in the middle of a busy freeway. I thought that I was going to die.

I knew I had to focus on my passion, my dreams and my family. I added faith to my determination.

I see the path to my success several and I am steps closer. I now enjoy the miracle of a successful business, my supporting wife, two loving daughters and the firm belief that miracles happen when determination is coupled with faith.

— Alfonso DeSoto

Forgiveness ... Setting One Free
Irene Kai

When I walked into the room, I was shocked to see Mother's condition. She looked helpless, lying there with a large tube snaking from the ventilator to her mouth, forcing oxygen into her lungs. Intravenous tubes wound down from a metal pole into her arms. My once almighty mother seemed so weak and small. Her grey hair reminded me of all the years that had elapsed since I had been the little girl who had tried her best to please her mother but to no avail. I was a grown woman and still her child. I felt safe in her presence for the first time.

I took Mother's hand and held it with both of mine. I whispered into her ear, "Mom, I am here." I searched her face for minute movements of facial muscles that might indicate she was trying to communicate with me, but her face was flat and calm. I closed my eyes and listened to the humming of the machines in the room and to her breathing.

A warm sensation washed over me. It was as if her life flashed before me. I realized that she had done her best. She had been unable to love and nurture her children because she could not function as a mature woman. She was forever that little girl who had never recovered from the devastation caused by her own mother's abandonment of her. Since birth, her mother had catered to her every whim, and then, suddenly, married her off to a stranger and a world she had never known, before disappearing to China. Nurtured by American society, she found herself ill-equipped to deal with the confinement of the Chinese culture or the aggressions from the men around her. She had lived her life precariously; her actions were determined by raw emotions without contemplating the consequences. She had been a wild mare in a glass house. I now understood that whatever damage she had done was not intentional. I just happened to be one of the innocent bodies in her tempestuous path. I squeezed her hand and nodded. I whispered in her ear, "Mom, I understand and I love you."

Her face seemed to soften. I stood by her bed and cried my heart out. It was as if my tears were washing away 44 years of pain and resentment. I felt grateful. I had finally found my way to forgive her and to love her.

I stood up and watched Mother struggle to inhale. I realized it was my forty-fourth birthday. It was as if she had waited for my birthday to give me the most precious gift, the freedom to live my own life. I closed my eyes and silently thanked her. She exhaled her last breath. Gone with Mother was the role of the punching bag. I straightened up and breathed deeply. I felt free and light. The weight of my family's judgments had lifted, gone with her forever.

— Irene Kai

Who told you to get comfortable?
Dr. Stephen Hudson

*O*ne of the biggest problems is that life is too easy. You don't have to walk five miles for clean water; you don't need to go hunting to feed you or your family, and you didn't have to build your home with your own two hands. Some people still have to do this but not you. You are lucky with a nice, cushy job, gadgets galore and a nice leather sofa. Life is very comfortable, isn't it?

Here in lies the problem. We spend most of ourlives in a "comfort-zone." We say, "I just bought my 42" surround sound TV, now my life will be that much better." Really?

In reality, the comfort zone isn't particularly comfortable and will result in constant challenges such as unexpected bills, poor health, and bland relationships. This is life's way of trying to get you to change because humanity, in its wisdom, likes the comfort zone. Mankind has invented distractions: you have to get that report done by Friday, can't do it tonight – Monday Night Football is on TV, I'll study for my test next week, I'll go to the gym tomorrow, I don't want to miss The Simpson's.

Distractions are a big problem. They include:

- TV, DVDs, videos, computer games, and Internet
- Alcohol
- Non-nutritious food
- Sports
- Gossip
- Holidays
- Gadgets and "must have items"
- Pornography
- Drugs – legal and illegal
- Sex
- Newspapers/magazines
- Trashy novels

I sound like a right-wing moralist, don't I? Well, as it happens, I am wearing my moral jackboots as I write this. Some of the distractions can be used to empower your life. The Internet can be an amazing source for research; sex is great, period, and holidays are part of enjoying life. They are called distractions because the vast majority of people engage in them to excess. Instead of deferring their pleasure, looking after their bodies and making enough money so that they can live the life of their dreams, they get caught up in excuses and distractions. The result is they end up living a mediocre life. Reject that half life; get passionate!

Assuming you want to change your life, is watching ER going to give you a better life? Wouldn't studying for that class get you to where you want to go a little quicker? You decide, because when you combine distractions with excuses, then we have the current comfort zone for most of the western population.

Now, no one is suggesting that you should remove all of life's pleasures. But you should not indulge in them when there are more beneficial things to do. You should not live your life for your pleasures. Pleasures should be your rewards. Don't live for the comfort zone. The problem is, in the long run, the comfort zone is far from comfortable. It is an illusion. Why? Life is a harsh mistress. She demands the best from her children, and if they don't live up to her expectations, she will make them suffer. The suffering is designed to get them to change their ways. This is, in the long run, for our own well being. Most of the time, we don't listen, and when we don't listen, we suffer.

— Dr Stephen Hudson

Don't Play it Safe
Rina Hafiz

*A*ll my life I played it safe. Our family motto was "better safe than sorry." In college I selected "safe" teachers, those in whose class I could get the "A." I got a nice, safe degree in electrical engineering, followed by a safe job with the government, safe relationships and so on. But there was a part of me wanting something more; I didn't know what I wanted, so I had no idea how to get it. I never would have guessed that "playing it safe" was to blame.

When the opportunity for a business in cosmetics, came along, something inside of me said, "Yes," without any analysis or thought. For once, I trusted my gut feeling. I didn't even think, "Do I really want to sell lipstick?" I was trying something new, and that longing for having more in my life started to be fulfilled. Naturally, with the new business, I played it "safe," by telling no one what I was doing. I worried about what people would think, and I settled for building with fear.

Even though I had become a success in business, I still refused to let go of a full time engineering position. Engineering was predictable, easy and secure. I convinced myself that it was good to have a safety net. Looking back, I realize now that the net was really over me instead of under me. It was a belief limitation keeping me from soaring higher.

I truly feel blessed for having the opportunity to start a business instead of staying with safe corporate America. Because of an extensive education, personal growth and the new skills I developed in my business, I now live the life I love. Building your own business forces you to face your communication flaws and overcome each one.

My original goal was to make enough to have someone clean my home. My husband felt having a maid was a waste of money. I vividly remember the first time our house was cleaned. We had a fine crystal chandelier in our dining room that we had bought in Prague; I came home that day to see my husband staring at the chandelier with all the lights on. I asked him what's going on. He said, "Did you know it's not frosted glass?" I looked at the lights and realized the glass wasn't frosted anymore. Since then, I haven't vacuumed in seven years, and the house is always clean.

Because I stepped out of my comfort zone, we were able to build our dream house on five acres. I have a gourmet kitchen for decoration purposes only because someone cooks for us. We have someone else mow the grass, but we play soccer on it with our kids. In kindergarten, my son had so many airline miles that he was getting credit card offers in the mail. I put my kids on the bus in the morning and am there when they get off in the afternoon. I get to go to the school when I want, go on any field trips I want, be secretary of the PTA and still make a great income. All I gave up was house work, constantly balancing my check book and living for Fridays. I put away the boring cars and earned a pink Cadillac!

I have always been great at money management. When I first started working as an engineer, I lived off of half of my salary. The rest I saved or invested. Later on when I got married, I lived off of one third of what I made. But even at that savings rate I would never have achieved what I have today. The reason for this is that, in business I learned how to set goals and reach them and having only one source of income that is so over taxed is no way to get ahead. Not only have I invested for college educations for four kids, but we are also giving back to our parents. And regardless of what our children or parents do with our gifts, I have learned not to be attached to the outcome of their decisions. Total freedom is knowing that you control your choices and allowing everyone else to learn from theirs. I am free from what others think, what they will say, or what they might do I have the luxury to only invest in what I think.

I remember staring at my cubicle walls one day and being so frustrated with my job that I wrote down a description of my perfect life. I wanted to watch the kids play on the swings while I worked on my deck, and work with only people I liked. After I wrote my description I remember looking out of the window and seeing people in the July heat keeping the lawns on the complex. I thought, "They are so lucky to be outside today." A few years later I read this description. I get to plan every day; I have more time to do what I want; I am the major influence in my kids' lives and can take a vacation anytime I want. Once you decide on the life you want, you have to find the courage to live it.

— Rina Hafiz

You Gotta Wanttta

Lee Beard

I remember it well; I can see it today as vividly as the day it happened.

It was during a presentation from a small-town basketball coach. He told a story about one of his championship players. It is a story of desire, and the miraculous changes that desire can make in our lives.

When he first saw her, three ideas were trying to balance themselves in his mind. First, he saw the potential for her to be a star, although less experienced coaches might have missed the tell-tale signs of future brilliance. Second, he noticed that she was overweight and out-of-shape; she had no business in sports – especially a sport that required constant movement and endless exertion. Third, he reminded himself that his was a small school in a small town, and the choices were few.

The story of chance is amazing. What if he had continued to look for some "perfect" player? What if he had decided that it would take too much work to convert this potential player into the real thing?

But the most powerful thing that I remember from his story was the result of his constant instruction; the interaction of the coach (teacher) and the player (student). When she found it difficult to run the simplest of drills, he told her, "You gotta wantta get from one end of the court to the other." It was the same at every practice: "You gotta wantta, you gotta wantta, you gotta wantta." It soon became her battle cry as she practiced and then, as she played: "You Gotta Wantta!"

The kid who wouldn't have been picked to play became a champion.

This had such an impact on me that I made a sign which reads (you guessed it), "You gotta wantta," and placed it on my desk. Even now, it seems to say it all: "You gotta wantta."

For some reason, it sums up the essence of passion. A little dab will do, but a whole lot more won't hurt you, either. Can you tell that I've become attached to that phrase?

As I go through the day, I often recall the words and the story. It brings a smile to my heart and a renewed determination to my spirit. I am reminded that "I gotta wantta" complete the task – no matter how tedious or commonplace or difficult – to get to the end of the project. Without that spirit of "gotta wantta," every obstacle is insurmountable; every challenge is a defeat.

I would wish for you the discovery of a passion that stirs your spirit and energizes your life so that each day is fun and each task is exciting. I believe that would make life better, and would make you a better person in the eyes of each one you meet. I hope to stir up your "wantta" so that you've "gotta" do it.

— Lee Beard

Author Index

Barbero, Robin...67
robin@conscioustalk.net
623 Old West Central
Franklin, MA 02038
508-541-0144

Beard, Lee 117
lee@wakeuplive.com
Lee is currently the Executive Producer of the #1 best-selling
series, *Wake Up ... Live the Life You Love.*

Chan-Cook, Kwai Lan..29
Lana168@earthlink.net
P.O. Box 443
Burbank, CA 91503
(818)640-6811
Kwai Lan is an imperial Feng Shui master and teacher. Her
system is unique and brings about more rapid results. She has
helped many transform their lives using Feng Shui.
www.imperialfengshui.com

Chopra, Deepak 45
The Chopra Center for Well Being
7630 Fay Avenue
La Jolla, CA 92037
Fax: 858-551-9570

Conard, Scott, MD...3
sconard@tienahealth.com
wakeupandlive@tienahealth.com
7200 North Hwy 161
Irving, TX 75039
(972)443-5300
President and Founder of TienaHealth; an integrated health
care facility adding years to the life and life to the years of
its patients by empowering them to take control of their
health. Services provided include lifestyle, weight loss, family
practice, chiropractic, massage, accupuncture, heart and sleep
medicine evaluations.
www.tienahealth.com

Cox, Serina 17
yogaserina@yogaserina.com
6333 E. Mockingbird Lane, Suite 147-674
Dallas, TX 75214-2692
www.yogaserina.com

Cummings, Carolyn 7
Essentialoils10@aol.co,
5588 S Parker Road # 155, Aurora, Co 80015
303-627-8808
Entrepreneur, Writer, Speaker, Classes
Events, Essential Oils, Handwriting Analyst
http://cummings.younglivingworld.com

Desoto, Alfonso 109
Entrepreneur
Co-Author, *Intelligent Stress – How to survive Stressful Times
at the Workplace*
adesoto@aboutstressmanagement.com
www.AboutStressManagement.com

Dyer, Wayne 5
Best selling author and lecturer
Author of *Real Magic, Manifesting Your Destiny, Pulling Your
Own Strings* and other books.
www.waynedyer.com

Fernandez, Peter G., M.D......................................23
DrPete@DrFernandez.com
1-800-882-CHIRO

Forster, Sandy 61
sandy@prosperitycoaches.com
Universal Prosperity Pty Ltd
P.O. Box 362, Mooloolaba
Queensland. 4557 Australia
61-7-5444-6186
Speaker, Entrepreneur, Mentor,
Author of the International program and Audio series
"Millionaire Mindset - 7 Steps to Your Financial Freedom"
www.prosperitycoaches.com
www.wildlywealthywomen.com

5421 Lynx COURT
Frederick, CO. 80504
303.702.0105
www.roselakecentering.com

rina@marykay.com
mybeautyanalysis.com

Genesis Business Development, Inc
9107 Champion Circle, Franklin, TN 37064
615 591-8003
GENESISBD@bellsouth.net
John Hall has had an adventurous career as an educator, sports
coach, owner of several small businesses and a consultant. He
currently divides his time between writing (children's books
are his favorite) and investing in the lives of his five children.
His driving motivation in life is to make a positive contribution to everyone with whom he comes in contact.

America's Ambassador of Possibility
Newport Beach, California
Co-author, *Chicken Soup for the Soul* and the *One Minute
Millionaire*
Founder of *"Goal-Mining Challenge"*
www.markvictorhansen.com

1700 NW 167th Place, Suite 220
Beaverton OR 97006
503-906-6001
A sought-after speaker, author, and workshop leader, Bill
Harris is Founder and Director of Centerpointe Research
Institute and creator of Holosync® audio technology. Started
in1989 with borrowed recording equipment set up on his
kitchen table, Centerpointe now has over 150,000 Holosync
users in 172 countries.
Centerpointe Research Institute
www.centerpointe.com

Isageniex Distributor. Chula's goal is to be the highest paid, most sought after woman motivational speaker in the world.

and travels throughout the country providing the course to those desiring a unique and complete understanding and practicality of how we can love ourselves and others more, and on purpose. He teaches individuals, couples, families, and companies. Matthew is also in the process of training others to provide the program. If you are interested in participating in the Mastery of Loving Program or becoming a trainer, you may find out more about Matthew and the *Mastery of Loving Program* by visiting www.MASTERYOFLOVING.com..

Creator #1 Best-Selling *Wake Up Live the Life You Love*
www.wakeuplive.com
562-884-0062

sylvia@thejoyofadulthood.com
The Buckhead Center for Health
3098 Piedmont Rd. NE, #430
Atlanta, GA 30305
404-237-7130
Sylvia is the founder of Buckhead Center for Health and Synergistic Explosive Success, SEXS. She is also an author, *The Joy of Adulthood: A Crash Course in Designing the Life You Want.*
www.thejoyofadulthood.com
www.sylviasays.com

sssykes@secondarycapitalnetwork.com
Naples, Florida

Positive Present
9663 Santa Monica Blvd. # 657
Beverly Hills, CA 90210
(866)270-0015
susyntimko@aol.com
Susyn is the CEO of Positive Present, a leading motivational company dedicated to helping children around the world.Our vision for 2024 is to help over 100 million children and families powerfully survive child abuse and neglect and to help

over 100 million children affected by drug and alcohol abuse and low self-esteem.Our grand vision, by 2044 is to eliminate the cycle of child abuse around the world. We will obtain these goals through our positive products.Visit our website to lean more about us and to purchase our products. www.positivepresent.com

Mentor to Millions
Success Expert
He is the author of the #1 best selling book, *The DNA of Success.* Jack was awarded the *Presidential Medal of Merit* by President George Bush and was honored by the United States Senate for teaching Americans how to achieve better results in their personal lives and careers. He was selected by *Winners Digest,* a publication for *Fortune 500* executives, as one of the two most effective speakers in the U.S. He is considered a *"Who's Who"* of *Human Potential Superstars* and the *"Best of the Best"* by *Nightingale-Conant.* Jack conducts seminars and customized training programs as well as life-changing retreats all over the world. His client list includes *Fortune 500* companies and associations of all sizes.